IRAQ AND DEMOCRACY

A Futuristic Perspective

Reza Rezazadeh

To the people of Iraq and those of other developing countries who aspire to a just society; to those exploited, alienated, made homeless and victims of poverty and injustice; and to those looking for a concept of a just society; to all those, this book is dedicated as a guide hoping that one day it will be understood by the common people and their aspirations will become materialized.

FIRST EDITION

Copyright 1993 by Reza Rezazadeh

Published by Eternalist Foundation
1080 Eastman Street, Platteville,
Wisconsin 53818 (608)348-7064

Manufactured in the United States of America
ISBN: 0-9629032-1-3

Library of Congress Catalog Card No.: 93-072961

Contents

the Revolutionary Command Council,
the National Assembly, the President
and the Cabinet, the Judicial Branch,
regional and local governments.

State constitution, the legislative branch,
the executive branch, the judicial branch.

PREFACE

It seems not only timely but pressing that the Western governments pay serious attention to struggles within the countries of the Middle East toward attaining a certain form of representative government. It is more likely that such attention will disclose the fact that democracy as applied and understood in the West may not be appropriate or even applicable to the countries of the region. With substantially different cultural backgrounds, some aspect of which being in sharp contrast with the Western values, democracy may take a quite different road yet be representative of the majority wishes and aspirations with the recognition of minority rights within the framework of the dominant cultural values. This is the starting point of a long way toward a true democracy. It cannot be expected more at its first stage and it should be considered justified. One should note that democracy is a societal phenomenon and requires time to be developed and integrated into the societal culture. When the Constitution of the United States established the national representative system, it limited substantially political rights of the majority of the citizens. Only the adult, property owning citizens were allowed to vote. All women were excluded, all slaves were excluded and all poor people were excluded. After property ownership requirement was abolished by the 1840s, political rights remained highly restricted for more than one hundred years until the 1965 Voting Rights Act was passed by Congress.

When the Bill of Rights was added to the Constitution in 1791, it did not apply to the states. Yet, nearly all american population lived within the state territories. All the states were left free to discriminate against and suppress the citizens rights as they wished. Why the Bill of Rights did not include, when proposed in the late 1780s, provisions to protect individual rights against infringements by the state governments? The obvious reason was that with such inclusion the Constitution would not have been ratified by the states. The society was not ready for it.

Even when the 14th Amendment was ratified after the Civil War in 1868, which made states responsible for the application of due process of law and equal protection under the law, the states did not follow. It took nearly sixty years that finally by the action of the U.S. Supreme Court states were forced to accept selective parts from the Bill of Rights. It took an additional forty years until nearly all the provisions of the Bill of Rights were imposed on the states by the Supreme Court rulings. Thus it took over two hundred years until the individual rights embodied in the U.S. Constitution became functionally applicable in the United States. This is a good example to illustrate the slow development and integration of democratic norms and processes into the national culture. The United States started with a very limited form of democracy and it took over two hundred years to reach its present status which is still substantially defective.

Looking upon the efforts of the less developed countries, like those in the Middle East, one must be patient and expect no miracles. As long as they show a continuous attempt to achieve a representative form of democracy the West must be satisfied.

From this standpoint, Iran is a good example. Iran presently has the best form of a democratic representative system in the Middle East, even better than Turkey. One will understand this by comparing the constitutions of both countries and the actual application of them in these two countries. The Turkish Constitution imposes discretionary restrictions by the government on human rights. An ordinary legislation can override most of the civil rights provisions of the constitution. In actual operation, Kurds in the southeast, a sizable population of the country, and Armenians in the northeast are highly suppressed. In Iran on the other hand, the Constitution is quite extended in civil rights. In actual operation the electoral process has been quite open for both sexes. Even the minority religious groups are guaranteed representation in Parliament by the Constitution based on the size of each. These include Armenians, Jews, and Zoroastrians.

In the past parliamentary elections over 82 percent of the eligible people voted. Twenty-two women were elected comprising 8 percent of the 270 total membership which is proportionally higher than women membership in the 435-member House of Representatives in the United States. Citizens aged 16 and over were eligible to vote compared to 18 and over in the United States.

A twelve-member Council of Guardians in Iran replaces the senate in the United States. Like the U.S. Senate the Council has veto power over the legislation passed by Parliament.

The Revolution allowed a full spectrum of Islamic leftist and secular ideas, supporting the Revolution, to flourish. The prerevolutionary parties were reactivated, including the Mojahedin and Fadayan. Several new parties were organized including the Islamic Republican Party (IRP) created by clergy loyal to Khomeini. Gradually all other parties were eliminated by IRP which rose in power and became a highly polarized elitist organization. It was finally dissolved by the consent of Khomeini in 1987 as a result of a joint request by Khamenei and Rafsanjani. This is an admirable step toward government by the people. The framers of our constitution did not consider political parties useful for democratic process but harmful to it.

The fusion of traditional Islamic ideals with political values during the first decade of the revolution resulted in the emergence of a populist political culture. It created a pervasive feeling that the government is obligated to ensure social justice and that it is the duty of every citizen to participate in politics. This is a giant first step toward democracy and has forced the leadership to express, constantly, its concern for the welfare of the disinherited and praise, persistently, the citizens' participation in a host of political and religious associations.

Mass political involvement has been an objective as well as a characteristic of post revolutionary Iran. Political parties were justly eliminated. Today, political participation is through religious institutions and voluntary associations. The mosque has become the most important popular political place. Participation in weekly congregational prayers at which a political sermon is always delivered is considered a religious as well as a civic duty. Several religious-political associations are centered on the mosques. These associations tend to be of a voluntary type where members devote several hours per week to related activities. The associations undertake a wide variety of activities such as checking the religious credentials of aspirants for local offices, distributing ration coupons, holding classes in a variety of subjects mostly for political orientation, setting up teams to monitor prices of goods and personal behavior. It is not only the mosques but factories, schools, even offices also have Islamic associations with similar undertakings within the community. Consequently, in Iranian communities, through these voluntary associations, people participate in ruling themselves outside of the sphere of the government as well as monitoring the appropriate functioning of the government.

Scientifically speaking, one can see in Iran a substantial development of democratic political culture within the framework of the Islamic religion. With over 95 percent of the country belonging to this religion, people feel much more comfortable with the Islamic system rather than facing and being forced to accept Western values many of which are incompatible with their religious beliefs and practices. This must be accepted as a fact in evaluating the nature and extent of democracy within the Middle Eastern societies.

Considering that the government is not only responsible but obligated to secure social justice, people tend to allow the government strength and unity to be able to carry out these obligations without strong organized opposition. They reserve this opposition right to themselves if the government does not perform properly. It was on this ground that during the last elections most of the hard liners were ousted from the Parliament leaving President Rafsanjani in a stronger position to carry out his obligations.

This approach may seem authoritarian from the view of the Western conception of democracy. But it seems that a certain degree of concentration of power in the executive branch is needed during the first stage of democratic process. The study of some other successful Third World countries like South Korea, Taiwan, and Singapore shows that some mixture of democratic-authoritarianism has been extremely beneficial to improve economic conditions first while laying the foundation of the representative system and then gradually achieving more political and civil liberties. Compared to the countries mentioned above, Iran has gone much further toward establishing a popular democracy. Many westerners not being familiar with the level of higher education in Iran may assume that the Parliament is composed mainly of clergy. Among the 270 members of the Third Parliament,

130 held university degrees (BA, MA, and Ph.D.). This was a 70 percent increase compared with the Second Parliament. The present parliament, the Fourth, has even more of these members even though the exact statistics are not yet at hand.[1]

Therefore, in evaluating the form of democracy proposed for Iraq all these cultural and religious factors presented above must be taken into consideration. One must also consider the historical experimentation with the Western democracy which has never worked and often has turned into harsh dictatorships because of the sharp cultural contradictions. Most of the Latin American countries are good examples.

INTRODUCTION

The main purpose of this study is first, to have a brief look at the historical experience of the Iraqi people and a variety of experimentation carried out in the short period of Iraq's independence. Second, through analyzing the outcomes of the old and new problems, diversities, aspirations and hopes of the Iraqi people, make a scholarly attempt to come up with a democratic system of government acceptable and applicable to the complex situation of a developing and ethnically diversified society like Iraq.

The study of the Iraqi society, with its diversities in culture, religion, classes, and language, proposes that the suggested political system in this study is the most apparent solution to the major problems of the Iraqi society. It sets the ground for bringing about a stable system inducive to individual and societal development. It is hoped that the proposal will be carefully and neutrally considered, analized, and evaluated. This is a rough and, more or less, general proposal. It is a starting step, though a fundamental one, for crystallization of an appropriate constitution for the nation as the foundation of its future.

This proposal is particularly of value to the opposition groups with their diversified objectives, ideologies, directions, and leadership. These groups, as it became evident during the Desert Storm War, will not be able to establish international or national credibility when they present fundamental disagreement with one another unless they can come up with a unified, solid, acceptable, practical, and promising

1

plan for the future of their country. This proposal, which lots of work has been put forward for its crystallization, offers such a plan by attempting to accommodate the major differences while leaving room for future and secondary compromises and reconciliations.

Since this writing is intended for the general public many technical and scholarly discussions necessary to clarify the points have been either avoided or presented in a simplified manner. It is obvious that scholars and experts based on their knowledge of theories of government and conditions of the Iraqi society, can draw their own conclusions from the structures and processes presented here. For the general reader, who may not have such a scientific background, attention to the forms, components, structure and functions of the government as presented here in their simple forms, will make sense. Simplification attempts are made to the extent of making the proposal understandable to a person with a normal general education.

This book is also directed to the American public which is usually quite uninformed or misinformed about the people, religion, and the way of life in the Middle East; Iraq only being an example.

The way of life in the Middle East is so complex and diversified that even scholars on the subject often disagree with one another, not arbitrarily or emotionally, but they do so based on their scientific background. This is usually labeled as scholarly disagreement. I have looked upon the subject matter from the viewpoint of a political scientist, an economist, and a legal scholar. From this standpoint, it is very understandable that some of my colleagues with expertise on the Middle East, Iraq in particular, may disagree with me. An historian, an economist, a writer, a sociologist, each will have a different vision of the same society despite the fact that there may be certain areas of agreement.

CHAPTER 1.

IRAQ WITHIN THE CONTEXT OF THE MIDDLE EAST

The Middle East has been the meeting place, often violent, of diverse ethnic, national and religious groups. In its narrow definition the Middle East embodies Egypt, Israel, Lebanon, Iraq and the countries bordering it. These are Syria, Turkey, Iran, Kuwait, Saudi Arabia, and Jordan. Figure 1-1 illustrates this regional subdivision.

The most significant geographical phenomenon common to all of the Middle East is the lack of water. An estimated 90 percent of the region is arid. Only about five percent of the area is cultivated, part of which needs irrigation. Since ancient times, preservation of water has been necessarily an important task. Different methods such as viaducts, cisterns, and underground canals have been used to preserve vater. The area is fed by only two major river systems. The Nile River, the longest in the world (4,145 miles), flows from the highlands of Central Africa and ultimately joins the Mediterranean Sea in Egypt. It irrigates about ten miles on each of its sides. It has been the source of life in Egypt and the fertile ground for the development of the ancient Egyptian Civilization. The Nile not only has provided water

Figure 1-1 The political map in 1986

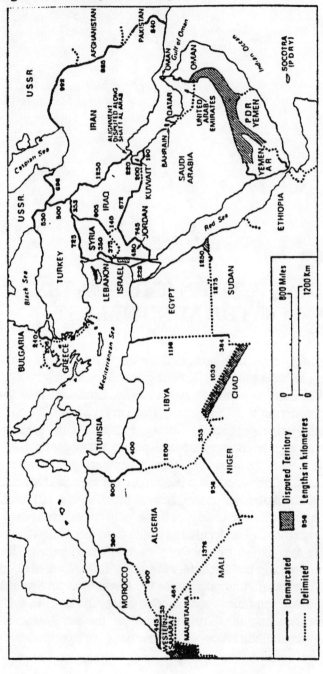

but also, through its annual flooding, has replenished the soil by bringing in and depositing millions of tons of extremely rich sediments.

The other major river system in the Middle East is the combination of two rivers, Euphrates and Tigris, both flowing through Iraq. These two rivers join together in the southern part of the country and form the Shatt al-Arab, which is the boundary between Iran and Iraq. Based on the 1975 boundary treaty between Iraq and Iran, this part of the river system is jointly used by both countries since the boundary line goes along the middle of the river system. These two rivers originate in the highlands of Turkey and then enter the territory of Iraq. The area between and surrounding these two rivers system is known as the Fertile Crescent, which was the center of the early civilizations. From the standpoint of the vital importance of water, Iraq is the most fortunate of all the Middle Eastern countries. Furthermore, while the Nile River has to feed over 60 million people on its shores in Egypt, the Fertile Crescent river system in Iraq nourishes only about 18 million. It provides not only abundance but also surplus.

However, it must be noticed that because of the scarcity of water in the whole region, any source of water, no matter how meager, is of vital importance and not infrequently the subject of violent encounters for its use. In this relation, there are rivers like Karun in southwestern Iran, Sefid Rood (White River) in northern Iran, and Karkheh in southern Iran, Kizel Irmak (Red River) in northern Turkey, the Jordan, Litani and Orantes rivers that irrigate parts from Jordan, Syria, Israel and Lebanon.

Except for portions of northeastern Turkey and the Caspian Sea shores in northern Iran, the rainfall is inadequate to support cultivation since most of the rainfall is in spring and winter; drought in the summer is a general expectation.

Usually, the climate is hot in summer and warm in winter in Egypt, Arabia, the Fertile Crescent, and parts of Iran. It is cold in winter and cool in summer in mountainous regions of Iran, Turkey and Lebanon.

It seems from the evidence that the Middle East region was once covered by forests. But today, it is deforested with a few exceptions such as the shores of the Caspian Sea and the Zagros mountain region in Iran, the southern shores of the Black Sea in Turkey and mountains of Lebanon. In these areas one may find the abundance of oak, pine, juniper and other trees. Because of the scarcity of grazing lands, the size of cattle is not significant and for the same reason the milk yield is quite low. Notwithstanding horses, mules and donkeys the most useful and distinguished animal in most of the area is the camel. It is still an essential part of the tribal life in the areas remote from modern roads. Besides transportation and a variety of domestic work, the camel is almost totally used for life support. It provides meat and milk, its hair is used to fabricate tents, rugs, and cloaks; its dung is used for fuel, and its urine to wash hair. Most countries of the Middle East produce wheat, barley, rye, lentils, onions, beans and some fruits such as pears, plums, apples and grapes. Persian peaches and melons, and dates of Iraq are world famous. Dates not only are a staple food for most of the people in the Arabian peninsula, but its pits are used to feed animals, the fiber of the tree turned into rope, and the wood for fuel. Overall, the Middle East does not provide enough food for its inhabitants. Among these, Iraq may be considered an exception.

Besides oil, the Middle East has scant mineral resources. The vast resources of oil in the region is mainly located within the four countries of Saudi Arabia, Iran, Iraq, and Kuwait. Because of the need of industrialized countries for oil the region since 1908, when oil was first discovered in Iran, has been a prime center of international intrigue and power politics. The ever increasing demand for oil is going to sustain this power struggle for well into the next century. The recent developments in oil politics do not solely relate to industrialized powers but also those countries in the region which lack oil and other resources and live under harsh economic conditions. These Arab countries are now demanding to share the fortunes of those blessed with enormous oil resources.

Another significant cause of international politics and super power interest in the Middle East is its prime strategic location. It connects the continents of Europe, Africa, and Asia. It borders the three major oceans of the world; Russia, a superpower, and China, with over a billion population and potential superpower.

The People

A great majority of the inhabitants of the Middle East are of Caucasian background. These comprise Iranians, Turks, Lebanese, parts from Egypt, Syria and Iraq. These are of the same stock as Italians, Greeks, Spanish, French and Irish. Negroid and Semetic people comprise most of the Persian Gulf region which includes all of the Arabian peninsula (Saudi Arabia, southwestern Iraq, United Arab Emirates, and Oman). However, the area peoples are differentiated, not much on the color of their skin and physiognomy, but by the difference in language. Aside from some minor dialogues, there are four major languages which sharply distinguish the peoples of the region. These, in order of population size, are Arabic, Turkish, Persian, and Kurdish.

The dominant Semetic language peoples in the Middle East are those speaking Arabic. These form separate contiguous countries. Despite their nationalistic, regional, and religious differences, they have linguistic and cultural ties. Other languages with a Semetic base are Hebrew spoken in Israel, and Syriac spoken by Assyrians. The latters are Christians and live mostly in Iran and Iraq.

Turkish is the second largest language spoken in the Middle East. This is not one of the ancient languages in the Middle East, but is rather new. It was brought by the Turks when they moved from the Far East into the Middle East. The Turkish language is spoken by the peoples of Turkey and Azerbiajan in the west, as well as Turkmans and Uzbeks east of the Caspian sea, comprising northeastern Iran and south central ex-Soviet Union.

The third major language, Persian, belongs to the Indo-European group. Historically, there is a linguistic tie between Persian and most of the languages of Europe and India. The Persian language is spoken, with some differentiations, in Iran, Afghanistan, Tajikistan (ex- Soviet Union) and parts of Uzbakistan (ex-Soviet Union), Turkmanistan (divided between Iran and the ex-Soviet Union) and Pakistan.

Closely related to the Persian language is the Kurdish, spoken in Kurdistan, which is divided territorially between Iran, Turkey and Iraq. The Armenians are another group related linguistically to the Persians, but they are Christian.

Islam

Islam, as the main religion of the peoples of the Middle East, is a vivid and important unifying force. Despite the fact that there are many different Islamic orientations and schools of thought, Islam is the strongest and deepest common experience of the peoples in the Middle

East. Islam, in its operation, is quite different from other major religions. It is not only a set of spiritual principles and goals, but is a way of life, not solely individual, but societal as well. It provides the institutions, laws, patterns, and the general environment, all devised to achieve and attain the basic goals of a homogeneous society.

Actually, Islam leaves little to the individual. Islamic laws attempt to prescribe and regulate each and every individual activity. For example, it prescribes the manner, direction, time, and sequence of daily prayers; has detailed laws regulating marriage and divorce, family property and its ownership and management, inheritance, economic and commercial transactions even rules for the act of war, the holy war, and maintaining peace. From the very beginning, using these religious ordains and guidelines, Muslims have fought others and one another, and built public institutions. It is utmost important to note that under Islam, the religion and government have been totally combined as one and inseparable from one another in practice. The specific bases for this unity will be presented later on.

It must also be noted that Islam and Arabism are two different and distinct phenomena. It is true that Islam was initialized by an Arab within an Arab society and was advanced into other neighboring territories by Arab conquests. Islam, however, does not coincide with Arab Civilization. Many of the modern Islamic countries that call themselves Arab, and aspire for Arab unity for political purpose, are not Arab at all. This kind of claim is especially confusing for those not familiar with the history of Islam as well as the peoples of the region.

Islam started with the bedouins of Arabia, but the countries they conquered, such as Mesopotamia (present Iraq), Egypt, Syria and Iran were not Arabs. The fact was that Koran, the holy book of Islam and the collection of all spiritual principles, was written in Arabic. This gave the Arabic language some air of holiness, especially by strict prohibition imposed on the translation of Koran, to any other tongue. Consequently, the Arabic language was imposed upon all conquered nations, since the ruling government used nothing but Arabic and encouraged no language other than Arabic. Ultimately, it became the medium of instruction as well as the official communication, and gradually it became a scholastic language and scholars in different periods produced their work in Arabic, regardless of their nationality.

By the passage of time some nations, such as Egypt, Syria, and peoples of North Africa, adopted Arabic as their language; some others, such as the Iranians, Turks, and Kurds, which never came to adopt Arabic as their language, discontinued to use it in their writings and scholarly productions.

It might be interesting to note that until the emergence of Arab nationalism during the last few decades, the term "Arab" applied specifically to the inhabitants of the Arabian peninsula; not everyone who spoke Arabic was considered to be an Arab. The pan-Arab concept did not receive serious attention until after World War II. Thus, the Arab unity is a modern political phenomenon rather than a historical one. With tremendous national and cultural diversity among the countries of the Middle East the Arabic language is a unifying force as much as the Islamic faith. Today, this is more evident than any other time in recent history of the area.

Islam has heavily affected the culture, the way of life and even the governmental institutions of the countries in the area. This very fact requires a brief look at some principles of Islam which have strong influence on the structure and operations of different societies in the region.

Islam is primarily based on the prescriptions of the holy book Koran. It consists of Muhammad's words claimed to be those of God spoken through his prophet Muhammad. Therefore, the Islamic religion evolved around what the prophet said or did.

To place ourselves in Muhammad's time and environment we need to take a brief look at the history of the time. There were two superpowers bordering Arabia; each controlled vast territories. To the northwest was the Byzantine Empire, controlling all of the Balkans (southeastern Europe), Asia Minor (Turkey), the eastern shores of the Mediterranean (Syria, Lebanon and Palestine), Egypt, and parts from North Africa (Lybia). Its capital was Constantinople, its official religion was Eastern Orthodox Christianity, and its language was Greek.[1]

To the east and northeast was the Iranian Empire, ruled by the Sasanids dynasty. They controlled vast territories on both sides of the Caspian Sea, the eastern part of the fertile Crescent (eastern half of Iraq), and the immensely vast territory located between Tigris (Iraq) and Indus (India) rivers. Their capital was Ctesiphone (on the Tigris river) in the winter and Ekbatan (Hamadan) in the summer. Their language was middle Persian called Pahlavi, and their religion was Zoroastrian. The government in both empires was autocratic (absolute authority of a single ruler) and religion was used as a tool of the state.

The Iranians were much more proud of their heritage, because theirs was more homogeneous, culturally and linguistically. These two superpowers were constantly at war because none was strong enough to achieve a definite and long lasting victory over the other.

Just before the birth of Muhammad, two great active and ambitious emperors ruled these two empires. Justinian (527-565) ruled Byzantium and the Sasanid Shahanshah (King of Kings) Khosrow Anushiravan (531-571) ruled Iran. During this period the two rulers, who called one another brother, concluded a peace treaty according to which Justinian paid 11,000 pounds of gold in order to be allowed to attack Italy. However, only a few years later, in A.D. 540, Anushiravan had poised his armies outside Antioch. In desperation, Justinian bought a five-year truce to 545 for some 2,000 pounds of gold, and finally, in 542, he agreed to pay 30,000 pieces of gold annually for a fifty-year peace. In 565, immediately after his death, hostilities were resumed between the two powers and continued thereafter.

During the various periods of peace, the two empires established diplomatic and commercial relations and engaged in cultural exchanges. The Byzantines developed art and letters and were deeply involved in theological issues. The Iranians supported and encouraged art and letters, advanced commercial transactions, particularly with India and China, and built magnificent edifices. More importantly, they developed a complete administrative organization for the empire which was later beneficially used for centuries by the Abasid dynasty of the Islamic empire. The Sasanians also established the famous educational institution of Gundi Shapur, comparable to the university institutions of today. Gundi Shapur became the greatest intellectual center of the period.

After Anushiravan, Iran was ruled by another great emperor Khosrow Parviz (583-628). Wars continued and for nineteen years the Sasanians swept everything before them and advanced as far as Damascus and Jerusalem. By 619 they had occupied Egypt, all Asia Minor, and were poised against Constantinople, the Byzantine capital.

During the reign of Parviz, Heraclius (610-641) another giant leader, came to power in Byzantium. In the same year, 610,

Muhammad was ordained by God to become His messenger. Heraclius continued to suffer defeat against the Sasanians and was obliged to spend his time preparing for war. Finally, in 622, Heraclius struck back at the Iranians and won victory after victory against the exhausted Sasanian army. To draw parallel with the development of Islam, this was the year that Muhammad assumed the status of prophet-king in Madina.

In 628, Heraclius stood at the gates of the Sasanians capital, Ctesiphon. The Emperor, Khasrow Parviz, was killed by his son and Heraclius got back all territories he had lost. However, the victory was an empty one, since both sides with years of war against one another, had exhausted themselves and had become ready prey for the freshly organized and highly motivated Arab forces.

Mecca, the Ka'ba, and the Birth of Islam

Mecca was the most important city in Arabia, located some fifty miles east of the Red Sea. Its prominence and prosperity were due to two factors: being on the trade route from South Arabia to the Mediterranean ports in the north, and the existence of the Ka'ba an ancient shrine that had gradually become the major religious center for most of the tribes in the region.

The Ka'ba made Mecca a holy city. It was a cubic structure with a black stone, considered holy, embedded in one of its corners. First, the neighboring tribes began to come every year to worship it. In the course of centuries, before the advent of Islam, its annual worship became universal among the pagan Arabs of the peninsula. Specific ceremonies and rituals were developed for this annual worship. Muslims believed that Ka'ba vas the place of Abraham and was built by him. They continued to perform the same religious rituals, though with different religious content.

As the Ka'ba grew in its reputation for holiness, Arabs while making their annual pilgrimage, brought their tribal man-made gods and placed them in the enclosure around the Ka'ba.

At the time of Muhammad, the political control of Mecca was in the hands of the Quraysh tribe. This tribe was in trade with Iran, Syria, and Egypt; they were not ignorant of the outside world as the other tribes. They were affected by the wars between Byzantium and Iran and had learned how to cope with the situation. They were also somehow aware of Christianity and Judaism, since there were Jewish and Christian tribes and settlements, in Arabia.

As a member of the Quraysh tribe Muhammad was born in 570 A.D. His father had died before his birth and his mother died when he was only six years old. He was cared for by his uncle, Abu Talib.

There is very little known about the early life of Muhammad. But, from the many stories, one can safely assume that he worked for merchants and traveled with caravans to distant lands, including Egypt, the Fertile Crescent, and Iran. These experiences made him quite familiar with different aspects of trade.

In 594, Khadija, a rich widow from the Quraysh tribe, was looking for a qualified man to manage her business. Muhammad was recommended for the Job. He was twenty-four years old, a member of the Quraysh tribe, and was known to be honest and experienced. He was employed by Khadija and a year later, upon her proposal, they were married. She was fifteen years older but had wealth and superior social status.

Because of this marriage, and his capability in business, Muhammad became a man of influence and prestige. For twenty-five years, he led a happy life at home and a prosperous business. Two sons and four daughters were the fruit of this marriage but the sons died in infancy. As the other rich men of his tribe, Muhammad had purchased and furnished one of the volcanic caves at Hira, near Mecca, in order to escape the heat and noise of the city. In the seclusion of this cave he often meditated.

It was in this cave that, after years of meditation, finally in 610, while fasting because of the month of Ramadan, he heard a voice which said to him "Recite in the name of the Lord who created, created man of a blood clot..." The night of this miraculous day was to be celebrated later as "The Night of Power."

Mohammed was frightened with this first revelation. He thought he was "possessed", despising himself so much that he thought to commit suicide. But his wife and her cousin greeted him with the interpretation that he will be a prophet to his people. After a while, Muhammad heard the voice again ordering him to "arise and warn". This made him certain that he was chosen by Allah as His messenger. The revelations were repeated at more frequent intervals. The concept of Allah (God) was revealed to him when he heard:

Say: He is Allah, the One!
Allah, the eternally Besought of All!
He begetteth not nor was begotten.
And there is none comparable unto him (Koran, sura 112)

For years, Muhammad preached the unity of God, as opposed to the polytheism practiced in Mecca. In the beginning not many followed him. The members of Quraysh, his own tribe, did not consider it a pride at having a prophet in their midst; businessmen saw economic ruin in his preachings; they saw the banishing of pilgrimage to Mecca and consequently the destruction of the city. Aware of this, Muhammad continued to preach his message.

In this struggle, as he gained formidable enemies, he was not in great danger since he was protected by his uncle, Abu Talib. In 619, his uncle died and his place was taken by Abu Lahab, who was an ardent enemy of Muhammad and his teachings. This year was also the year he lost his beloved Khadija. This brought the heaviest pain upon his life and, for the first time, he thought of leaving Mecca. Ultimately, he chose the city of Yathrib, about 200 miles to the north of Mecca.

The city had developed problems, and tribal rivalry, and was looking for an experienced arbiter from the outside. Muhammad became this much needed arbiter. They were familiar with his message and knew about the animosity between him and the other leaders of his tribe, Quraysh. Besides a new prophet, the people of Yathrib thought of Muhammad as a man of ability, familiar with the inner operation of an important tribe like Quraysh, and with the capability of leading the city in its rivalry with Mecca. Initial relations were established in 620, and continued until 622 when he was invited to go to Yathrib. Muhammad first sent small groups of his followers, including two wealthy men from his tribe, Umar and Uthman. He, then, together with Abu Bakr, his father-in-law, Ali, his cousin and son-in-law and his two wives, left Mecca secretly and entered Yathrib about September 24, 622. This became an important day in the history of Islam and became known as Hijra, which means the emigration. A few years later, this year was chosen as the beginning of the Islamic calendar. The city's name was changed to Madinat al-Nabi, or the city of prophet, and then was simplified to Medina, alone.

What followed in Medina established a very important principle in Islam which was followed, and today is an inseparable part of the Muslim faith. This was the principle of the unity of the religion of Islam and government. In Medina, Muhammad was the prophet of Allah as well as the head of the government. He had to act as a chief administrator, legislator, and judge, combining all three branches of the modern government into one. He thought to be responsible for the welfare of the community and its people. In practice, his complex duties as a political leader, overshadowed his role as a prophet. Apparently, for him and his people, the two offices were necessarily combined. Therefore, his legislative, judicial and executive actions were not considered solely coming from him, but being the solemn commands of Allah. As a prophet-king, he united government and religion. The spiritual, and the temporal, became inseparable. This practice instituted Islam as a theocratic institution in which religion and government merged into one. This principle continued in theory and often in practice as is revitalized today by the fundamentalist groups in Iran and some other Islamic countries. It is based on this principle that the present rulers in Iran justify the inseparability of Islam and government. All the legislation and temporal directions in Koran are considered to be the commandments of Allah for the regulation of daily life in an Islamic community.

This has created a big dilemma in Islamic societies. On the one hand, the modern Muslim finds the details of his life prescribed by his religious directions; on the other, by the importation of the Western, non-Muslim system of government, he is directed toward the separation of religion and state. For a true Muslim, it is very difficult to adjust himself to this new concept, which is so contradictory to his religious beliefs. The principle of inseparability is even, though indirectly, reflected in the constitutions of many Islamic nations when Islam is recognized as the official religion of the country.

To Muhammad, Mecca was the center of the Muslim world and this had to be established. At the time of prayer, every Muslim faced toward Mecca. However, he could not bring the city under his command until after several military ventures. When he ultimately entered his native city as a victor, he ordered the destruction of all the idols around the Ka'ba and made it forbidden to pagans. Instead of the house of gods, it became to be known as the house of God. He then returned to Medina, his political capital. However, Mecca became and remained, the religious capital of Islam. Muhammad, soon thereafter, became the acknowledged Messenger of Allah and the ruler of the whole Arabia.

During his ten years rule in Medina, from 622 to 632, Muhammad was engaged almost continuously in war. The wars were religious and explicitly for the purpose of establishing the rule of Islam. Apparently, for this reason, he personally participated in most of them. After his death in 932, he left behind a community which was at the same time religious, and an armed encampment. The religion was without a hierarchy or clergy. Every Muslim was also a military conscript; the leader in worship was also a military commander. The houses of worship, therefore, were at the same time the courts of law and the military command headquarters. It was under this Islamic concept that, during its war with Iraq in the 1980s, Iran was able to have over six million volunteers under conscription.

The Nature of Islam

To Muslims, Muhammad is solely the Messenger of Allah. Muslims are not the people of Muhammad but the people of the Book, namely the Koran, which embodies the message of God. This is essentially different from Christianity where Jesus as a person is the center of attraction. For this reason, the word Islam means "submission" to the will of Allah. It has no reference to Muhammad. A Muslim is the one who has submitted to the will of Allah. Some argue that, under this definition, a Jew or a Christian is also a Muslim since each also submits to the will of God. Therefore, ultimately it may be summarized that Islam is submission to the will of Allah as revealed by His messenger, Muhammad, and embodied in the holy book of Koran. This definition is very important and essential since it prescribes that every Muslim has to live under the jurisdiction of Allah and follow in all his actions, the laws and directions prescribed by Allah embodied in Koran. The proper interpretation and explanation of these laws form Shari'a which has become the most important guide for action in Islam.

A Muslim believes:

1. That there is only one God (Allah), who is the supreme creator and the sole source of guidance. This belief is the main source of the strength of Islam.

2. In many prophets, that Allah sent to guide His people in different times and places. Among these, Muhammad is the last. They begin with Adam, and continue through others such as Abraham, Moses, Jesus and end with Muhammad.

3. In the Holy Book of Koran. He also believes that each prophet Allah sent also had a Book, which embodied His direction for guidance of His people. From this standpoint, Koran includes all that one needs to know for guidance. Thus, in all ideas, beliefs, practices and institutions he must follow the Koran. Based on the concept of multiplicity of prophets, the peoples of a Book should not be forced to accept Islam; they should be allowed to follow their own faiths under the protection of Islam.

4. In the final Day of Judgment, in Heaven and Hell. In these regards his beliefs are much the same as Christians.

5. In angels, as creatures of Allah, who worship Him and are assigned to record individuals actions and be witness on the Day of Judgment. He also believes in angels who have turned against God, such as "satan."

To a Muslim, despite these beliefs, the practice of his religion is most essential. For this reason, these practices are known as pillars of Islam. There are five major pillars:

1. The Witness, which is the statement of the creed of Islam in one sentence: "There is no God except Allah; Muhammad is the Messenger of Allah." To witness the faith, this is used in many aspects of a Muslims life. The utterance of this sentence also is sufficient to admit a nonbeliever into Islam.

2. Prayer, which must be carried out five times a day, in prescribed intervals. Though these prayers have certain prescribed structure, they are purely individualized and are carried out by each Muslim wherever convenient. Islam does not have any institutional hierarchy or priesthood. Each individual is independent in his faith. There are men of religious knowledge of different degrees, the highest being titled as Ayatollah. They have no institutional authority, but are an authority on Islam and Koran. They are there to advise people when they have a religious question.

3. Giving or Zakah, which is an obligatory giving, similar to a tax levy. Zakah is besides voluntary giving and provides the government with funds to take care of its expenditures. The voluntary giving collected by the government or community are kept in a special account called wagf and is ordinarily used for religious and educational purposes.

4. Fasting, which is carried out during the month of Ramadan. This is the ninth month of the year, which was holy for the Arabs before the advent of Islam and continued to be thereafter. The fast is during the day time and the night is spent in keeping vigil, praying, and reading the Koran.

5. Pilgrimages to Mecca, which is required from every Muslim if he can afford it. This is known as hajj. The rituals are the same as they were before Islam. Each year, during the month of Zihajjah, the last month of the Muslim calendar, many thousands of Muslims from many parts of the world make this pilgrimage. This annual union gives a sense of solidarity to the Muslims and is very uplifting for each faithful individual.

Some Muslims also consider jihad (holy war) as the sixth pillar of Islam. The word jihad means struggle, as is mainly referred to war within one's own existence, soul against ungodliness and evil. Its reference to actual war comes from the fact that all wars in early periods of Islam were assumed to be struggles against the enemies of God and ungodly people.

CHAPTER 2.

IRAQ, HISTORICAL BACKGROUND

The intention here is not to go extensively into the historical background of Iraq. That will occupy several volumes that are already in existence and available through libraries. The purpose here is to introduce the general reader to a brief historical background that we deem necessary for a proper and better understanding of the present societal composition, as well as the foundation for cultural direction of the country and expansionist aspirations of the rulers, apprehension of our proposed democratic political system and future possibilities.

Ancient Mesopotamia

The history of the territory, within the present boundaries of Iraq and its people, dates back more than 5000 years. It could easily be called the cradle of early civilizations. The history of Iraq is also tied to two major rivers, the Tigris and Euphrates, and adaptation of the people to their ebbings and flowings. Initially, for a long time, these rivers were marked by an unchecked flow of water, causing inundation and destruction. But, once they were controlled by irrigation systems and other methods, they become the cause of fertile territories and abundance in food supplies. This quite vast area was later labeled as the Fertile Crescent. This fertility, abundance, and surplus of food, combined with an unfriendly and often harsh environment of the neighboring territories, induced people to move into these fertile lands and provided the ground for early civilizations. The famous ancient cities of Sumer, Babylon and Assyria, all were installed and flourished, within this environment. Besides these three major centers of civilization, the history of the territory is full of various autonomous and self-contained social systems. As a matter of survival, each of these autonomous units attempted to take appropriate security measures for protection against invasions from the outside. This has been a very important characteristic of the land. It has created a strong, decentralizing force in the culture of the territory. One important and peculiar factor helping this diversity of authority, was the lack of access to stone within most of the territory. Therefore, roads could not be built and, as a result, different parts of the country remained beyond the reach and control of the central government. This lack of roads and access, in many parts of the territory, is even evident today.

Different leaders in the period, extending to over 4000 years, have attempted to unify different peoples of the territory and preserve the civilization. Outstanding among these, were Hammurabi (1792-1750 B.C.), Cyrus of Iran (550-530 B.C.), Darius the Great of Iran (520-485 B.C.), Alexander the Great of Greece (336-323 B.C.), the Islamic Abbasid Dynasty (750-1258). Despite these efforts, Iraq's history has continually shown the conflict between the fragmented political authorities and the central government. For some 600 years, after the collapse of the Abbasid Dynasty in the mid thirteenth century through the end of the ottoman Empire in the early twentieth century, there was no sustained central authority over the territories; thus, political units, mostly tribal, remained effectively autonomous.

Early Mesopotamia

Historically speaking, the present Iraqi territory comprises what was known as Mesopotamia, where the ancient civilizations were born. If we go back about 8000 years (6000 B.C.), we find Mesopotamia inhabitants people who had migrated from the Turkish and Iranian highlands.

The river valleys of southern Mesopotamia, because of its fertility and the production of surplus food, perhaps for the first time in history, attracted migration of people from neighboring and less resourceful lands. At the same time, the volatility of the two rivers, Euphrates and Tigris, and ensuing destructive and disastrous floods required a form of collective management to protect the marshy, low-lying, but highly fertile lands. These collective actions led to urbanization and evolving of the Sumarian civilization in southern Mesopotamia.

Because of the multiplicity of ethnic groups, Sumerian culture became a mixture of foreign and local norms and habits. Perhaps, because of the formidable challenges created by the changeable climate of the two potentially violent rivers, Sumarians developed to be highly innovative and creative people. As the first civilization, they brought about great innovations and left behind great legacies such as writing, irrigation methods, highly developed agricultural systems, the wheel, literature, and astronomy.

Religion, in Sumer, took a rigorous shape with the emergence of a powerful priesthood which observed ritual practices and even could intervene with the Gods. The Gods, which personified natural forces as well as local elements, were to provide the individual with security and prosperity but this required sacrifices and adherence to prescribed rituals. Since all property belonged to the Gods, the priesthood made all decisions relating to land and agricultural questions, trade and commercial relations, as well as war.

The emergence of large cities and urban life led to more technological advances. For example, they advanced brick technology, which enabled them to build magnificent edifices and temples called ziggurat. They invented the wheeled chariot and bronze, by amalgamating tin and copper. These two inventions became a very important technology in warfare.

The history of Sumer starts from about 3360 B.C. and goes through many phases, during which different conquerors ruled the area and attempted to unify it. For example, Sargon I, King of the Semetic city of Akkad (2334 B.C); Hammurabi, King of Amorites, a Semetic people from the west (1792-1750 B.C.), with Babylon as their capital. He was famous for what became to be known as the Code of

Hammurabi, which was designed to provide justice and destroy evil. It regulated many aspects of social and property relationships such as land tenure, rent, contracts, administration of justice, labor conditions and wages, the status of women, marriage, divorce, and inheritance.

About the seventeenth century B.C., a group of tribes from Central Asia, known as Arians, invaded Iran and India and then moved westward. These tribes together formed what became known as Indo-European people. Stretching from India in the east to Europe in the west. The Hittites, which belonged to these groups, took over Babylon and by mid fourteenth century B.C. they controlled a wast area stretching from the Persian Gulf to the Mediterranean shores.

After the fall of the Hittites, Babylon was occupied by the Assyrians, though for a brief period, in the thirteenth century B.C. Later, in the ninth century B.C. the Assyrians expanded to the west and reached the Mediterranean Sea.

In 612 B.C. the Medes and the Chaldeans, allied together, defeated the Assyrians and the Chaldeans became heir to Assyrian power and reestablished Babylon as the most magnificent city in the region. The famous Hanging Gardens of Babylon were created during this period. In 539 B.C., Babylon was conquered by Cyrus the Great (550-530 B.C.), Achaemenid emperor of Iran. He freed the Jews held captive in Babylon.

Up to 550 B.C., Mesopotamia had been under the rule of different Semetic-speaking people for some 2000 years. From this point in time, it fell to Indo-European hands, which lasted some 1,176 years. Cyrus was a great and conscious leader. He replaced the cruelty of the Assyrians, with respect to the culture of his new subjects. After a brief instability after Cyrus's death, another outstanding Iranian emperor, Darius the Great (520-485 B.C.), brought about political stability. His efficient and innovative administration created a period of great economic prosperity.

Between the death of Darius in 485 B.C. and the conquest by Alexander the Great in 331 B.C., Mesopotamia fell into decay. Babylonia and Assyria, still part of the Iranian empire, became economically isolated and thus impoverished. During some 200 years of Iranian rule, a large number of Iranians moved into the area creating an important demographic trend, which has continued with different intensity up to the present. Iranian rule also caused the disappearance of various languages spoken in the area. They were replaced by Aramic, which was the official language of the Iranian empire.

The victory of Alexander the Great in 331 B.C. was short lived, since while returning from an expedition to India, he died in Babylon in 323 B.C. He was then only 32 years old. Political chaos followed his death and his empire was divided and ruled by his generals, who fought among themselves until 126 B.C. when the Parthians, another intelligent people from Central Asia, after conquering Iran, captured the Fertile Crescent. They retained the existing social institutions and enriched the area. With some short interruptions Parthians ruled the area until A.D. 227 when it was conquered by the Sassanids, the new native Iranian rulers. They ruled for over 400 years, during which the continuous wars between the Romans and Sassanids not only effectively weakened the Iranian forces, but also destroyed the territory. By A.D. 636, when the weakened Sassanid empire was conquered by Muslim Arabs, the area was in ruin as a result of the wars and government neglect of the canals and irrigation facilities. The ancient Sumero-Akkadian civilization had been entirely extinguished. A couple of years after Muhammad's death, during the last year of the rule of Abu Bakr (632-634) the first caliph and the father-in-law of Muhammad, the Muslim Arab forces advanced into Mesopotamia and defeated the exhausted and enfeebled army of Iran. Umar, the second caliph (634-644), sustained the well organized and centralized Iranian administration, tax assessment and collection procedures, control of income and expenditures and bookkeeping. Arabic replaced Persian as the official language and slowly but gradually became of common use. Iraqis were converted to Islam and intermarried with Arabs.

All the Sassanian empire was conquered by Muslims by 650 and thereafter the efforts became concentrated on managing and maintaining these territories.

Sunnis and Shias

Who was the rightful successor to the office of the Prophet Muhammad? This soon became the subject of controversy. The focus of attention was Ali ibn Abu Talib, the cousin and son-in-law of Muhammad, opposed to Uthman the third caliph. Ali spoke on behalf of the tribal volunteer soldiers who had fought the wars but had not received the benefits from them. He also criticized the new innovations in practice not in compliance with directions of the Koran. Discontent mounted. Uthman was besieged in his home and slayed. Ali, who was not involved in the siege, was designated as the fourth caliph. After a sharp division and battles between opposing Muslim forces Muawiyah, a relative of Uthman who was declared caliph in Egypt by some of his followers, and Ali remained as the caliph in Iraq, Ali was ultimately assassinated in 661. For his followers he became "Lord of All Martyrs", and the sect of Shia was crystallized. Shias believed of Ali the rightful successor to Muhammad, as the first caliph. Besides Muhammad, Ali came to have the greatest impact on Islamic history. His name was added to those of God and Muhammad in Shia declaration of faith: "There is no God but Allah; Muhammad is His Prophet, and Ali is the Saint of Allah".

After Ali, Muawiyah was declared caliph and Damascus became the capital of the Umayyad Dynasty which followed. After Muawiyah's death in 680 his son, Yazid I, became the caliph. Ali's second son, Hussein, refused to pay homage and was asked in Mecca to lead the Shias against the caliph. The plot was discovered and at Karbala, in Iraq, Hussein's group of some 200 men and women refused to surrender to some 4000 Umayyad troops and were killed. Hussein's death, on the tenth of the month of Muharram, became established as the day of mourning for all Shias. It is known as *Ashura*, and is observed with rituals and devotion. Karbala, the burial place of Hussein, and An Najaf, that of Ali, both located in Iraq south of Baghdad, became, and remaine, holy places of pilgrimage for Shias.

These events created the greatest division in the Islamic world. The followers of Ali became known as Shias and those of Muawiyah as Sunni's, or people of the Sunna who follow Muhammad's customs and ways of life. Therefore, Shias view themselves as the opposition minority who are against privilege and power. They consider Muawiyah, and his dynasty the Umayyads, as usurpers who gave Islam wrong direction. They see in the lifestyle of Ali the true practice of Islam, and a just cause in Hussein's sacrificing his life. These two role models have inspired Shias to struggle for social and economic justice.

The Abbasids (750-1258)

The Iraqi and Iranian dissenters who had fled to Khorasan (northeastern Iran) gradually formed a faction that supported Abd al Abbas who had a distant relation to Prophet Muhammad. In 747, they were able to attack the Umayyads and occupy Iraq. In 750, Abd al Abbas became the first caliph of the dynasty, known as the Abbasids. Arab and Iranian cultures mingled in Baghdad during the rule of early Abbasids. It produced the sharp flourishing of science, philosophy, and literature. Baghdad grew rapidly and became the nerve center of trade linking wast areas together. The irrigation systems were developed by harnessing the two rivers and large quantities of food was exported.

Intellectual pursuits were actively supported, particularly during the reign of Harun ar Rashid (786-806) and his son, Mamun ar Rashid (813-833). The abbadids were Sunnis, but initially received the support of Iranian Shias. Disappointed, they started to rebel by the 820's and break away from Abbasid rule. Several local dynasties ruled Iran.

The Abbasid caliphs imported Turks as slave-warriors, known as Mamluks. They guarded the imperial palace, but, gradually, because of their military proficiency and dedication, they occupied high positons at court. Their influence increased to the extent that by the tenth century the Turkish commanders actually appointed and desposed caliphs. They kept caliphs because of the importance of the office as the legitimate source of authority and power. In 945, a Shia military group from south of the Caspian Sea known as Buwayhids, occupied Baghdad but continued to allow the Sunni Abbasids caliphs to rule. The caliphate was manipulated by Shias and Iranians until 1055 under another Turk group known as the Seljuks. They were Sunnis and thus treated the caliphs, still figureheads, with respect.

Seljuks let Iraqis and Iranians rule and administer their territories and pay tributes. During this period Iran and Iraq witnessed a scientific and cultural renaissance, particularly under Malek Shah, led by his Iranian grand vizier Nizam al Mulk, known for his brilliance and unique administrative skills. After Malek Shah (1092) the Seljuk dynasty disintegrated. In 1219, Chinggis Khan, a powerful Mongol leader, with his large and savage army moved into central Asia, devastating cities on his way and often slaughtering every living thing. By 1227, the year he died, he had reached western Azerbaijan in Iran. After Chinggis's death it did not take long until his grandson, Hulagu Khan, arrived. In 1258, he conquered Baghdad and killed the last of the Abbasids caliph. He massacred all the capital's scholars, intellectuals, and religious leaders and constructed a pyramid from their skulls. He destroyed anything relating to a civilized society, including canals and irrigation systems, scientific and literary works. Iraq became a devastated frontier province while the Mongols made Tabriz in Iran their capital. In 1401 Baghdad was sacked and its inhabitants massacred by another Mongol, Tamerlane. He devastated hundreds of Iraqi towns, killed their inhabitants and built pyramids of skulls. Under his rule, Islamic arts and scholarships were virtually extinguished everywhere in the region.

As a result of devastating Mongol invasions, Iraq plunged into political chaos, social disintegration, and economic despair; Baghdad and Basra lost their commercial and political importance. Destroyed irrigation systems caused a rapid deterioration of agriculture and Iraq regressed from its urbanized civilization to tribal settlements of the river valleys, pastoral nomadism and continued as such well into the twentieth century.

From 1534 to 1918 the course of Iraq's history was subject to the continuing conflicts between the rulers of Iran and those of the Ottoman empire. Iraq was important to Shia Iran because of the Shia holy places, such as An Najaf and Karbala. It was important to Suni Ottoman Turks to contain the spread of Shia Islam to Anatolia, their central territory. In this struggle, ultimately the Shia inhabitants of Iraq suffered, by being excluded from politics as well as economic developments.

By the beginning of the twentieth century, the Ottomans had failed to control Iraq's rebellious tribes. The insecured situation also led to the growth of self-contained and autonomous communities. All these were formidable obstacles toward creating a nation state. By this time also Iraq, along with other Ottoman territories, had become the focus of European power politics and rivalry. British vital interests in India, Iran, and the rest of the region and intrusion of Germans supported by the Ottoman Young Turks, significantly increased British interest in Iraq as part of its vital lines of communication. Besides occupying Baghdad in 1917, during the first World War, the British extended their authority to all Iraq by the end of the war with the exception of the Kurdish highlands.

At the 1919 Paris Peace Conference, Iraq and Palestine were mandated to Britain, and Syria to France. The British had many problems of establishing administrative authority which the most significant was the growing anger of the nationalists who felt betrayed and were demanding independence. The British faced continuous rebellions and as a result, in 1920, replaced the military regime with a provisional Arab government, assisted by British advisers. This government was composed chiefly of Sunni Arabs leaving, as in previous occations, the Shias highly underrepresented. In 1921, the British chose Faisal as the first king of Iraq. He was the son of Hussein ibn Ali, sheriff of Mecca and thus, was not considered an Iraqi but a British creation. The continuous inability of the government to gain public confidence created political instability. In this process, Iraq's new military force, because of its good organization and discipline, gained increasing power and influence. It was Sunni dominated, since its high ranking officers were Sunni, who had been trained under the Suni Ottoman system.

The Anglo-Iraqi Treaty of 1921 established a new framework of a parliamentary monarch system. The most pressing issue for the new government was the question of boundaries, especially relating to the Kurdish province of Mosul in the north. The Treaty of Sevres, which was concluded in 1920, between the British and the Ottoman ruler, prescribed that Mosul was to be part of an autonomous Kurdish state. The treaty was abrogated by Mustafa Kamal (Ataturk), a nationalist and the first ruler of the newly established Turkey. By the use of force, he established control over the Kurdish areas in eastern Turkey. Thereafter, there were two attempts by the British to establish an autonomous Kurdish territory, but both failed. The ultimate decision was to include the Kurds in the new Iraqi territory with the condition that they will be designated to governing positions in Kurdish areas. The Kurdish language also was to be preserved.

The League of Nations, in 1925, accepted the Mosul area as part of Iraq but proposed that, as a protection for the Kurdish minority, the term of Anglo-Iraqi treaty be extended from four to twenty-five years, with due regards to Kurdish culture and language. It was ratified by Iraq in 1926. As a result, the vast oil resources of the area came under Iraqi authority within an area to be controlled by well armed Kurdish people.

Iraqi politics took on a new dynamism with the struggle for power between Shia and Sunni leaders. Wealthy and prestigious Sunni families in the cities, and Ottoman trained military officers and bureaucrats, had the upperhand. However, those seeking power lacked legitimacy, because the government was created by a foreign power and, furthermore, Iraq gained no experience with the democratic concept of government. Accordingly lacking supportive constituencies for a democratic process, despite the constitution and an elected assembly, Iraqi politics became subject to varying alliances of important personalities.

The nationalists' opposition to the Anglo-Iraqi treaty continued through 1920's, with a demand for an unconditional independence. It finally became materialized in 1929, when the newly elected Labour government in London recognized Iraq's independence. On October 13, 1932, Iraq became a sovereign state and was admitted to the League of Nations.

Problems After Independence

Scores of complex problems faced the new government relating to social, economic, religious, ethnic, as well as ideological conflicts; intense competition for power began between Sunnis and Shias, urban people and tribes, Assyrians and Kurds, and nationalists and traditionalists. The centuries old Sunni-Shia conflict became a formidable obstacle to form a unified political entity. This conflict was further intensified when a disproportionate number of Sunnis occupied governmental positions. There were, of course, much more Sunnis with administrative training and experience under the Ottoman system. Shias, economically suppressed for a long time, wanted also to have a voice on economic issues.

The Kurds and the Assyrians, who had hoped for an autonomous status, opposed their inclusion within the Iraqi state. Kurdish hostility and drive for autonomy remained a serious problem for the Iraqi government.

Assyrians staged armed resistance which was put down by a Kurd, General Bakr Sidgi. This marked the military's entrance into politics and passage of a conscription law, which further strengthened the position of the military.

The first military coup in the Arab world occurred in 1936, by General Bakr Sidgi. During the reigns of King Faisal who died in 1933, his son Ghazi (1933-39) who was killed in 1939, and his son Faisal II who was executed by the revolutionaries in 1958 Iraq continued with its socioeconomic, cultural, ethnic and religious problems. Most important among these were the post W.W.II socioeconomic conditions. The shortages caused by the war and inflationary prices provided for further opportunity for exploitation of the masses, sharply widening the gap between rich and poor. The income of the salaried middle class such as civil servants, military officers, and teachers depreciated continually. The peasants were the worst off under the control of the wealthy land owners. These continuing disparities and hardships in the 1950s and the 1960s provided opportunity for the Iraqi Communist Party (ICP) to strengthen its roots among the people. At the same time, the nationalist movement considered the monarchy as a British puppet, under the control of the apparent British servant, and Iraqi strong man Nuri as Said.

From Monarchism to Republicanism

In July 14, 1958, by a swift coup, the group of Free Officers led by Brigadier Abd al Karim Qasim and Colonel Abd as Salaam Arif, overthrew the monarchy. The coup, which considering its consequences may be called a revolution, met virtually no oppostion. Both King Faisal, along with many others in the royal family, were executed and Nuri as Said was killed while attempting to escape disguised as a woman. It is worthy to note that the July 14, 1958 Revolution was the culmination of accumulated grievances which had led to a series of coup attempts starting with Bakr Sidgi in 1936. The Revolution responded to people's grievances by radically changing the social order. The power of the large landowners was curtailed, and the conditions of the workers, the peasants, and the middle class were improved. Relieved from the years of suppression, conflicts between Kurds and Arabs as well as Sunnis and Shias resurfaced.

Qasim, perhaps influenced by his poor origins, improved worker's conditions and brought about land reform aimed to unseat the old feudal landlords. He also established ties with the communists, which caused an attempted coup by a group of conservative Free Officers against him. In 1959 Qasim concluded an extensive economic agreement between Iraq and the Soviet Union. The Baath Party decided to eliminate Qasim, Saddam Hussein was designated for the job. Qasim, though injured, escaped the assassination. In the meantime, by 1961 the Iraq Communist Party (ICP), extending its strength among the people and its influence in the government, had become too strong obliging Qasim to check its power. He eliminated the ICP members from sensitive government positions, cracked down on trade unions and farmers associations. Alienating the communists and the nationalists and conflicts between the military made Qasim's position vulnerable.

The Kurds, who expected equal treatment based on the new constitution put forth by Qasim after the 1958 revolution, continued being discriminated against. Ultimately, in 1961, full scale fighting broke out between the Kurds and the government forces and ended with the inability of the government to put down the revolt. This further undermined Qasim's position. His tendencies toward the left deteriorated his position further by turning the regional leaders, particularly the Shah of Iran, against him. He was overthrown in 1963. However, he remained a hero to millions of poor people.

Strongly pitched battles followed between the communists (ICP) and the Baath Party; ultimately the Baath was able to consolidate power and establish the National Council of Revolutionary Command (NCRC) as the top policy-making body. But beleaguered by internal division, in 1963, the Baath was overthrown by Abd as Salaam Arif who transferred the management of the country to the armed forces. His efforts to form a union of Iraq with Egypt, the latter being ruled by Gamal Abdul Nasser, changed by 1965 and Nasserite activities were curtailed. Arif was killed, in 1966, in a helicopter accident and his brother General Abd ar Rahman took the office with the approval of the National Defense Council.

In 1968, the Baath Party manipulating a military coup materialized by Colonel Abd ar Razzag an Nazif and Ibrahim ad Daud, took over power again. By this time the Baath Party was much better organized and determined to stay in power and to focus on pressing domestic issues. As its power base the party created a militia of its own and an intelligence organization. By this time also, the party's ruling elite was a close family and tribal clique more notably from Tikrit, a Sumi Arab northwestern town. Three of the five-member Revolutionary Command Council (RCC) were from Tikrit; Ahmad Hasan al Bakr, Hammad Shihab, and Saddam Hussein. The positions of president, prime minister, and defense minister were controlled by Tikritis. From 1968, when the Baath took over the power to 1973, the party ruthlessly eliminated any group or individual suspected of opposing the Baath rule. This was done through a series of sham trials, executions, assassinations, even intimidation. To further legitimize and institutionalize its rule, the party issued a Provisional Constitution which granted the Revolutionary Command Council extensive powers. As it will be discussed later, this constitution, with some modifications, is still in effect today.

Being associated with the army and the nationalists, Bakr brought the Baath Party popular legitimacy and support from the public as well as the military. Saddam Hussein, becoming increasingly dominant, experienced in organizing clandestine activities, outmaneuvered the opposition, and eliminated his political opponent who he deemed necessary. By 1969, he had become the moving force behind the party. Under his leadership, to penetrate the Iraqi society, the party established a complex network of intelligence and grassroot organizations and extended the size of the party militia.

Because of becoming ill and also facing other family tragedies, starting in 1975, Bakr gradually relegated his powers to Saddam Hussein. By 1977, all important institutions of government, instead of Bakr, reported to Saddam Hussein. To Saddam Hussein, the Revolutionary Command Council and the cabinet were only rubber stamps for his policies and decisions. In 1979, when President Bakr resigned, Saddam Hussein became not only president but also chairman of the Revolutionary Command Council, and commander in chief of the armed forces.

Besides, other international problems, the most serious and continuing danger facing the government was the Kurdish unrest in the northern part of the country. In 1970 the government made a peace and autonomy agreement with Mustafa Barzani, the leader of the Kurdish Democratic Party (KDP). Though agreement brought about immediate pacification, it was not completely satisfactory because of the uncertainty of the territorial boundaries. The Baath attempt in 1974, to assassinate Barzani and his son Idris, caused full scale fighting to break out. Kurds, received aid from the Shah of Iran and the United States, both wary of the Soviet influence in Iraq.

Saddam Hussein found it necessary to reach an agreement with the Shah. The result was an agreement signed, in 1975, in Algiers. The agreement recognized the thalweg (approximately the middle of the waterway) as the boundary in the Shat al Arab and dropped all Iraq's claims to southwestern Iran and to the islands in the Gulf. This was a quite significant concession from the part of Saddam Hussein. In return he received the Shah's agreement to prevent subversive elements from crossing the border, which actually meant no Iranian assistance to the Kurds. It resulted in the defeat of the Kurdish forces, known as Pesh Merga, most of which surrendered under an amnesty plan, some defied the plan and remained in the mountains to continue to fight, and some crossed the border to Iran, joining over 100,000 Iraqi refugees there. A year earlier, in 1974, Saddam Hussein had proposed to the Kurds a quite comprehensive autonomy plan. The plan recognized the Kurdish territories, Kurdistan, as an autonomous area to be governed by an elected legislative assembly and an executive council with its president to be appointed by the Iraqi president. This area government was to have control over local and area affairs. The only execeptions were defense and foreign relations, which were to remain central government functions. However, this autonomous region did not include the oil rich, but Kurdish area of Kirkuk. But at the same time, Saddam Hussein attempted to weaken future Kurdish resistance by relocating, by force, a substantial segment of the Kurdish population from their heartland in far northern Iraq, which resulted in razing all Kurdish villages along some 800 miles of the border with Iran. Apparently, such brutal relocation activities renewed guerilla attacks and the autonomy plan did not materialize. During this time also, conflicts in strategy and policy determination among the Kurdish leadership reached the point of split in the unity of command. In mid-1975, Jalal Talabani formed a new organization called the Patriotic Union of Kurdistan (PUK) which was mainly urban based and more leftist oriented than the Kurdish Democratic Party (KDP) led by Barzani.

When Barzani died in 1975 his two sons, Idris and Masud, took over the KDP; in 1979, Masud was chosen chairman of the party who proclaimed continuation of the armed struggle against the Baath. However, the split in leadership and the intra-Kurdish struggles significantly inhibited the effectiveness of the struggle.

After successfully putting down the Kurdish rebellion in 1975, Saddam Hussein turned his attention to socioeconomic issues mainly for consolidating his domestic position. Based on the socialistic oriented ideology of the Baath, Saddam Hussein followed a state sponsored industrial development plan. The plan caused a tied relationship between many middle class Iraqis and the Baath party. With the Baath's consolidated power, these and other economic policies (1976-1980) were successful. They caused a greater social mobility, a wider distribution of wealth, a better access to health care and education, and a land reform and redistribution. The success of the socioeconomic programs was very much due to the sharp increase in oil prices in 1973 and the following years, which provided funds necessary to carry out the programs.

Parallel with these developments at the home front, Saddam Hussein also pursued an ambitious foreign policy with the aim of establishing Iraq as a leading force in the Arab world. A very important side of this policy was to establish a secured and friendly relationship with Iran, highly populated with a strong military might. This aim was almost attained through the 1975 treaty with Iran. Now, he could try to improve relations with Saudi Arabia and other Gulf states as well as Syria and Jordan. His position for Arab leadership was suddenly and tremendously enhanced when Egyptian President Anwar Sadat concluded the Camp David peace accord with Israel in 1978, and consequently Egypt was ousted from the Arab League.

But history had a disaster in store for Saddam Hussein. In February 1979, the Revolution in Iran overthrew the Shah and replaced it with a theocratic government of fundamentalist Islamic Republic led by one of his arch enemies, Ayatollah Ruhollah Khomeini. Not only Saddam Hussein lost security of his eastern borders as well as the strength of his own position by the elimination of the Shah, but establishment of a fundamentalist Shia government in Iran was even a greater danger for the stability of Iraq, where Shias constituted the majority of the population (estimates vary from 55 to 70 percent of the population). In the first place, the Baath followed a secular rather than a religious ideology; and secondly, Saddam Hussein, apparently to please the Shah, had expelled Khomeini from Iraq after living for 13 years in Iraq, in the Shia city of An Najaf.

The Iranian Islamic Revolution brought to the surface Shia dissatisfaction with the Baath government and caused organized religiously oriented opposition. The Iranian strategies to expand and export Islamic fundamentalism rapidly deteriorated Iraqi-Iranian relations. In July 1979, just a few months after the Iranian Revolution, riots broke out in the Shia centers of Karbala and An Najaf in Iraq. The leading figure was Ayatollah Muhammad Bagir as Sadr, an inspirational Shia leader of the group named Ad Dawah al Islamiyah (the Islamic Call).

Apparently, early in 1980, Saddam Hussein planned for war with Iran. In March, 1980 he terminated diplomatic relations whiten Iran and immediately thereafter, along with a series of intimidations and accusations, the government rounded up the leading supporters of Ayatollah Bakir as Sadr. Saddam Hussein ordered his execution, along with his sister. Thousand of Shias of Iranian origin, dubbed as the "fifth columnists" were deported to Iran. In late August, there were skirmishes around Qasr Shirine and other border lines. By early September, some 130 square kilometers of Iranian territory were occupied by the Iraqi forces. In mid-September, Saddam Hussein officially abrogated the 1975 treaty and extended the sovereign power of Iraq over whole Shatt al Arab. A few days later, on September 22, full scale invasion against Iran took place.

The Iranian government was caught off guard when the invasion started and Iraqi troops moved into Iranian territory. Border outposts were undermanned and were not in a position to defend themselves against well equipped armed forces prepared for offense. Furthermore, at this time, the Iranian clerical regime had not been well established and was facing substantial internal group conflicts. In the military front, the armed forces were intentionally decomposed by the fundamentalist regime by executing many of their upper rank, seasoned and experienced officers and by fleeing from the country many more of their capable commanders. The situation was further complicated by the formation of the Revolutionary Guard as a counterpart to the armed forces. Apparently, seeing Iran in disarray with a headless, disorganized, armed force and inexperienced and non-professional Revolutionary Guard troops, Saddam Hussein found a unique opportunity to materialize his ambition by a full scale offensive.

However, the extent of his miscalculations became evident during the first ten days of invasion. Though the Iranians were caught by surprise, Iraqi advances were substantially slowed down by fierce resistance and defense of the local forces. Iran hurriedly organized its forces and stopped the Iraqi advances. After about a year of stalemate, in 1981 the Iranian forces started counter offensives and pushed the Iraqis out of the territory. There were some three years of stalemate, despite repeated Iranian attacks against well entrenched Iraqi forces. Finally, there were significant Iranian advances into Iraqi territories, nearly in all fronts and then retreats, when Saddam Hussein resorted to extensive use of poison chemical weapons. At the time of the truce in 1988, there were some minor territories in the hands of Iraqi forces.

This was a war extremely costly to both sides. An estimated one million were killed and much more injured and disabled. Economically, both countries were devastated but the cost for Iraq was much heavier because of the phenomenal increase in its foreign debt, used to pay for its war machinery. By one estimate, the cost of war for Iraq was around one billion dollars a month. From a social viewpoint, destruction of hundreds of cities and villages permanently affected people's way of life.

After the truce with Iran, Saddam Hussein mobilized Iraqi's communities for reconstruction of whatever was destroyed. But the consequences of the Iran-Iraq War were disastrous to the Iraqi people. It altered the course of Iraq's history by causing severe dislocations in the economy, placing the country deeply in foreign debt, by one estimate around 80 billion dollars, and straining social as well as political life.

During over some two years between the end of the war with Iran and the invasion of Kuwait on May 2, 1990, the resolution of socioeconomic problems took the backseat in contrast to the military buildup. A substantial part of the national income was spent in upgrading the weapon systems and employing high technology and modern processes.

However, the disastrous consequences of the war with Iran resulting from Saddam Hussein's miscalculations apparently did not serve notice to be more cautious in planning to invade Kuwait. Controversies between Iraq and Kuwait mounted; first, about billions of dollars Iraq owed to Kuwait, mostly borrowed to pay for the war, and Iraq wanted these to be written off; second, about the oil field of Rumaila where more than nine-tenths of the oil reserve is located in Iraqi territory and Kuwait was extracting oil from the corner of this wast reserve, extended into its territory. Saddam Hussein considered Kuwait stealing Iraqi oil and wanted the extraction to be stopped; and thirdly, about long term lease of the two islands of Bubiyan and Warba to Iraq, since Iraq did not have convenient access to the Persian Gulf. When Kuwaiti responses were not satisfactory, Saddam Hussein, with the impression that the United States and Europe would not interfere, committed another miscalculation and invaded and occupied Kuwait, without much resistance from the part of the Kuwaiti armed forces.

Contrary to Saddam's calculations, the invasion brought immediate response from the United States which tried to create an alliance with other European countries and unite members of the United Nations Security Council. The United States' efforts caused the Security Council to declare and impose a total embargo against Iraq, embodying all exports and imports. In the beginning, it was hoped that the sanctions would force Iraq to withdraw from Kuwait. But, during the following six months, Saddam Hussein demonstrated firm intentions to keep Kuwait as a province of Iraq. By December, the United States president had decided on military action and imposed his decision on the Security Council by convincing its permanent members to go alone. Only Cuba and Yemen voted against military action and China obstained. The war started in mid-January, 1991. In order to make the war a Middle Eastern affair, the United States bought Egypt's participation by writing off seven billion of its debt, and showed rapproachment to Syrian president with whom the U.S. government had no positive relations. But, all the alliance members had a token participation, Egypt having the largest contribution of some 50,000 strong forces. Saudi Arabia, which was under immediate danger of Saddam Hussein's expansionist plans, necessarily became the host country. In a couple of days, allied forces established air supremacy and from there on it became a one-sided campaign with devestating results.

In reality, the war was a disaster for Iraq, the region, as well as for the allies. A devastated Kuwait was liberated from Iraqi forces to be returned to another harsh dictatorship; there was no real liberation. The war also did not attain a reasonable objective. Saddam Hussein remained in power to massacre tens of thousands of his own people.

Though both sides have a vested interest in covering up the figures, estimates coming from informed Iranian sources put the number of Iraqis killed at 160,000. But the figure for those who have died after the war and will continue to die as the consequences of the war is much greater. The Iranian sources reported daily death figures for nearly two million refugees around 10,000, caused by hunger and epidemics. One source estimated that the under-five child mortality will be 170,000.

The damage to the intrastructure of the country was monumental. It included electricity, water, seweage, health care, agriculture, the highway system, communication, major industries, and other essential resources of life. Despite all arranged 24 hour efforts, by the end of May, 1991, the electricity output was only 22 percent of its prewar level. By the end of July, there was substantial shortage of medical supplies and food.

At the time of this writing, the civilian Iraqi population faced severe malnutrition and unsanitary conditions resulting in cholera, typhus, meningitis, hepatitis and other diseases. Simply, hospitals and laboratories could not function properly without food, electricity and medical supplies. The mistake done by waging war, rather than continuing sanctions, will be haunting the conscience of the countries involved and will undermine, in particular, the credibility of the United States for many years to come.

Looking at the actual situation, the continuation of sanctions has cut off essential food, medical and humanitarian supplies punishing the civilian population while leaving the oppressive and aggressive regime intact.

CHAPTER 3.

THE PRESENT POLITICAL SYSTEM AND ITS FOUNDATION

After the coup d'etat in July, 1968, the Baath Party took over the power. To legitimatize its rule and the legality of its actions and institutions it proclaimed on July 16, 1970, the Provisional Constitution which embodied the three principles advocated by the Baath Party namely Arab unity, freedom, and socialism. The constitution being provisional allowed the rule by decree during the period of transition until the objectives of a democratic socialism were achieved with Islam as the state religion. The first principle, Arab unity, was to bring eventually together all Arab countries under a universal Arab system, "the Arab Nation," with a single leadership. It was understood that a permanent and properly modified constitution was to be enacted at the end of this transitional period. However, no specific time period or achievement of certain specific circumstances were established as criteria for the termination of the transitional period.

Ideological and Political Directions of the Baath Party

To understand the structure and functions of the government as well as the formulation of the Provisional Constitution, it is necessary to have a brief look at the development and objectives of the Baath Party.

In 1947, a group of Arab intellectuals devoted to the unity of Arab societies under one nation, met in an official congress in Damascus, Syria. The concept was initiated and advocated by two Syrian intellectuals Michel Aflag and Salah ad Din al Bitar recognized as the fathers of the Baath movement. Accordingly, the Baath Party took the form of all-Arab organization working within each Arab country toward unification. The Iraqis who attended this congress became the party members and immediately after their return to Iraq established what was conceived to be the Iraqi branch of the Baath Party. Abd ar Rahman ad Damin was selected to be the first secretary general of the party.

The Iraqi Baath started recruiting its members from among the educated youth in the high schools, colleges, professionals as well as military colleges. However, during the 1950s the party was obliged to go underground and join another clandestine opposition party under the unified name of the United National Front which was instrumental in the 1958 revolution.

The new regime led by Abd al Karim Qasim, was dominated by military officers who were not Baathists and did not support the Baath's united Arab objective. The party then plotted Qasim's assassination in which Saddam Hussein was involved. The attempt, in 1959 failed. Baath had to go underground again.

Four years later, in 1963, the party attempted again to overthrow Qasim and succeeded. The first Baath government was established. But because of the lack of unity of purpose within the party, the other coup partners who did not belong to Baath Party took over the power and in less than a year all Baath members were expelled from the government. Within this time and 1968, the party reorganized itself under the leadership of General Bakr. Saddam Hussein gradually became second in command.

The coup of 1968 established the Baath Party power firmly through its attempts to create a unified Iraq by expanding consensus through a variety of programs of general appeal. A new way of life was introduced based on the principles of socialism which embodied the elimination of exploitation and social inequalities, collectivism, political and social participation, free education, and national loyalty. Socialization of the economy continued during the 1970s and 80s, even though during the latter decade it was hampered as a result of the Iran-Iraq War. During these two decades, particularly in the 1970s, a significant part of the national economy was socialized, such as oil, major industries and commerce. Agriculture was also collectivized during the 1970s until it was abandoned in 1981.

For its membership the Baath Party was not interested in quantity, but quality. It was quite selective in choosing its members. The purpose was to form a knit organization with the ability to organize people, to administer effectively and efficiently not only the party programs and functions, but also the government. The attempt also was made to create a deep sense of loyalty and responsibility.

The hierarchical organization of the party and its functions at each level was carefully designed based on a centralized power concept (Figure 3-1). At the summit of the party hierarchy was the Regional Command. This was the top decision-making body composed of eight members and a secretary general all elected for a five-year term by the party Regional Congress. There was also a deputy secretary general who was second in command. In theory, the Regional Command was responsible to the Regional Congress which convened once each year to review, debate and approve policies and programs proposed by the Regional Command. But in its actual operation the members of the Regional Command were nominated by Saddam Hussein or other senior party leaders of his confidence, and then as a matter of formality the Regional Congress would elect them which in turn would give legitimacy to the leadership.

In the original structure of the Baath Party, there was also a National Command superior to all regional commands acting as a coordinating body and the highest policy-making command throughout the Arab world. Its membership consisted of representatives from all regional commands of different Arab countries. Its powers were to be exercised by a national secretariat.

However, in practice this has not happened and there is no unity or cooperation between different regional commands of the Baath Party. In fact, the Baath parties of Iraq and Syria are arch rivals which has

Figure 3-1. The Hierarchical Structure of the Baath Party

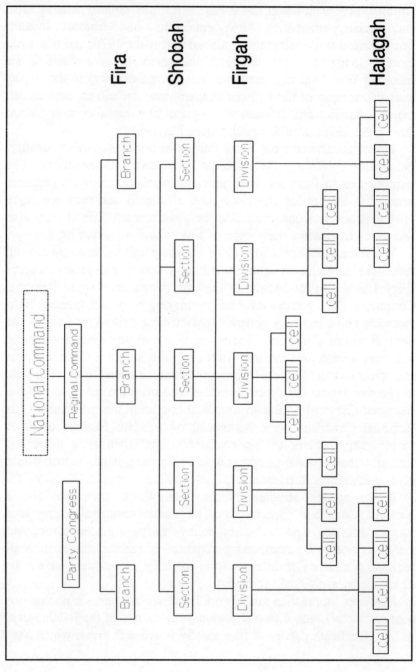

resulted in the creation of two rival National Commands, one in Baghdad and the other in Damascus.

According to the rules, the Regional Command in Iraq was to make party decisions, but in practice, all decisions were made and are being made by Saddam Hussein who has been the secretary general of the party since 1979, the chairman of the Revolutionary Command Council, as well as the president of the country. He functions through the loyal assistance of a very small group of supporters nearly all of these being from his home town of Tikrit and some his close relatives.

The party and through it the country was and still is ruled quite autocratically. He has dealt ruthlessly with the opposition, even those slightly suspected. Since he has taken power in 1979, many high ranking members of the party, also often in high positions in government and the military, have been executed with or without staged trials.

In 1974, the Progressive National Front (PNF) was created in order to bring the Baath and other political organizations in Iraq under one umbrella. Among these were the Iraqi Communist and various Kurdish political parties. However, by the late 1980s the Baath Party actually controlled the PNF. The Baath held half of the total seats, held nearly all executive positions, and pushed through the PNF rule that required all decisions be made by unanimous vote. All these together provided for a monopolistic control of the PNF by the Baath.

Despite PNF, the Baath did not tolerate political opposition. Because of powerful security and secret police systems, these parties were obliged to go underground or operate from the outside of the country. One of these operating in exile was the Supreme Assembly for the Islamic Revolution in Iraq (SAIRI) which was a union of the Iraqi Shia parties under one command. Its headquarters was, and still is, Tehran, Iran. Its objective has been to overthrow the Baathist regime and bring about a revolutionary Islamic republic.

The Consequences of the Baath Rule

In 1990, before the invasion of Kuwait, Iraq was no closer to democratic rule than it had been in 1968 when the Baath took over the power. Political activities were strictly restricted to those prescribed by the Baath. Any opposition or deviation was harshly and ruthlessly dealt with. All radio and television broadcasting was controlled by the government.

There were six national daily and seven weekly newspapers all published in Baghdad. Despite the fact that Article 26 of the Provisional Constitution guaranteed freedom of opinion and press within the limits of tho law, these newspapers along with books and other publications were subject to close censorship. All writings had to be in line with the nationalist and progressive objectives of the revolution.

The Provisional Constitutional Framework

As stated previously, the governmental system of Iraq is based on the Provisional Constitution adopted on July 16, 1970. Its major provisions are as follows.

Principles of Ownership and Production

The constitution is based primarily on the theory of revolutionary socialism directed ultimately for the realization of the pan-Arab economic unity. On the basis of this "scientific and revolutionary" theory, the state is empowered to plan, direct, and guide the economy. The Constitution defines all the basic means of production as well as national resources as the property of the people directed and exploited by the state, on behalf of the people, in compliance with the directions and procedures prescribed by various plans to develop the national economy. In this regard public properties and properties of the public including national resources are inviolable. Property ownership is defined as "a social function that shall be exercised within the limits of society's aims and the state's programs in accordance with the provisions of the law." This provision vests on the state a nearly limitless power to manage the economy and nature of ownership particularly when the government is autocratic and the "laws" are promulgated under a single controlling political authority like the Baath Party. This power over the ownership, production, and commercial functions is further enhanced when the Constitution guarantees private and individual economic freedom "within the limits of law." Again, if the government is controlled by a single power "the limits of law," could become unlimited. This shaky economic freedom is further hampered by a provision of the constitution prescribing that individual ownership cannot contradict or be detrimental to "general economic planning." Of course, the Constitution maintains the state's eminent domain right. According to this principle, private property can be expropriated only for the public interest and with just compensation. At the same time, for the purpose of land reform, the Constitution prescribes the size of private agricultural land ownership to be prescribed by law, and the excess to be taken by the state as the property of the people. There is no mention of just compensation here. Unless legally exempted, real estate ownership is prohibited to foreigners.

Individual Rights and Freedoms

The fundamental rights, freedoms, as well as duties of individuals are embodied in Articles 19 through 36 of the Constitution. Among these are freedom of religion, speech, press, and assembly; freedom to travel, privacy of correspondence and the inviolability of individual and of residence. The individual is also guaranteed right to fair trial and due process of law.

Right to free education is insured to every citizen from elementary school through the university level. As a first step in this direction, the Constitution prescribes the state to eliminate illiteracy. However, Article 28 of the Constitution states that the aims of education include developing conscious opposition to "the doctrines of capitalism, exploitation, racism, Zionism, and colonialism". This provision is obviously for the purpose of achieving the Baath Party's three principal aims of freedom, socialism, and Arab union.

The Constitution recognizes the right for employment and requires the state to provide employment to every citizen. It also guarantees free health care.

Governmental Structure and Functions

The Constitution establishes a governmental system consisting of three branches of the executive, the legislative, and the judicial, with corresponding checks and balances. However, in practice none of the other two branches have been independent of the executive. The following constitutional description of the executive powers clarifies the reason.

The basic organs of the government consist of the Revolutionary Command Council, the National Assembly, the President, the Council of Ministers, and the judiciary, Figure 3-2 illustrates a simplified hierarchical structure of the Iraqi government.

The Revolutionary Command Council

The Revolutionary Command Council was first instituted in July, 1968, and since then it has exercised both executive and legislative powers. When the Provisional Constitution was written and adopted two years later (July, 1970) these powers were legitimatized by embodying them in the Constitution. Article 37 of the Constitution establishes the Revolutionary Command Council as "the supreme body in the state." It has, according to Article 43, authority to promulgate laws and regulations by a two-thirds majority vote of its members. Its constitutional powers include: legislative, both in collaboration with, and independent of, the National Assembly; national defense and internal security; declaration of war and general mobilization to carry it out, and conclusion of peace; ratifying treaties and other international agreements: approval of the national budget. To guarantee the Baath monopoly, Article 38 prescribes that all members of the RCC must be elected from the members of the Baath Party Regional Command. Furthermore, the chairman of the RCC is also the President of the Republic and the commander-in-chief of the armed forces. The size of the RCC has varied over time; in 1990 it consisted of ten members.

By the Constitution, the RCC is given the responsibility of carrying out the "popular will" by removing from power the reactionary, eliminating dictatorship as well as the corrupt elements with the aim of returning power to the people. Each member of the RCC is answerable only to the RCC. Any member, including the chairman and the vice-chairman, may be dismissed by the council by a two-thirds majority vote. Any member also can be impeached and be charged of wrongdoing and made subject to judicial proceedings. The council establishes the rules for impeachment of its members who are

Figure 3-2. Government Organization, 1988.

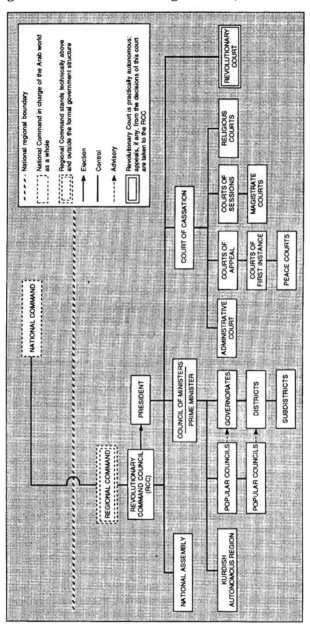

Source: Helen Chapin Metz, *Iraq: A Country Study,* Federal Research Division, Library of Congress, 1990, p. 180.

tried by the special court set up by the RCC for this purpose. Except for the legislative power, the council may delegate some of its powers to its chairman or vice-chairman. The chairman presides over the council's sessions, signs all laws and decrees issued by the council. He is also the head of the state.

To consolidate its monopoly of power, since 1977, the Baath Party has practically merged its Regional Command Council and the Revolutionary Command Council by considering all members of the Regional Command Council also as members of the Revolutionary Command Council, the former being the highest party policy-making body at the national level and the latter the highest policy-making body within the government. By this interlocking leadership system, the government and the Baath Party have become the one and the same top policy-making authority.

The National Assembly

The Provisional Constitution of 1970 called for a National Assembly as the legislative branch of the national government. However, this assembly was not actually created until 1980. Apparently, during the early years of the Baath rule since 1968, the RCC filled in for the legislative body since it could promulgate laws without reference to the legislative body. The law creating the National Assembly was issued by RCC in March, 1980, and the first election was held in June of that year.

According to the law promulgated by the RCC, the National Assembly consisted of 250 members to be elected by secret ballot every four years. To be eligible to vote one had to be an Iraqi citizen and over 18 years of age. The country was divided into 250 electoral districts, each with a population of about 70,000. The law prescribed a single electoral list with one representative to be elected from each electoral district. The qualifications of the candidates were subject to scrutiny and approval by an election commission appointed by the government. This appeared to be another instrument of control by the Baath regime.

To be qualified as a candidate for the National Assembly one had to be at least 25 years of age, be an Iraqi citizen by birth and from an Iraqi father, and not be married to foreigners. Therefore, having a non-Iraqi mother could be made grounds for disqualification. An exception was when the mother was an Arab and from another Arab country. Excluded were individuals who had been subject to property expropriation as a result of the land reform or nationalization laws. Above all, the candidates were required to satisfy the election commission about their belief in the Baath Party's revolutionary objectives, apparently, another means of the Baath control.

When the first Assembly convened in 1980, the Baath candidates occupied 187 seats or 75 percent of the total seats. This was securely over two-thirds majority required for special legislation. The remaining 63 seats belonged mostly to the parties allied with the Baath and some to independent parties. In the Second National Assembly, in 1984, the Baath party held nearly the same percentage of the seats namely 183 or 73 percent of the seats. Saddam Hussein was elected chairman of the Assembly. There were 33 women elected to this assembly, an unusual achievement of political right for women in an Arab country.

The National Assembly holds two 60 day sessions each year starting in April and November. It carries out its legislative duties along with the RCC. In fact, the legislation is proposed by the RCC and it is to the assembly to ratify or reject it. As it has been demonstrated the assembly is controlled by the Baath Party and therefore, it can be properly assumed that it acts as a rubber stamp for the RCC. The assembly has limited authority to pass laws on its own if it is proposed by a minimum of a quarter of its membership. In this case also it is clear that no measures in opposition to or in conflict with the Baath policies will be approved by the assembly dominated by the Baath Party. The assembly also has the function to ratify the government's budget and international treaties. In these and all other areas as well, the ultimate legislative decisions is made by the RCC.

The Presidency and the Cabinet

The Provisional Constitution does not prescribe a term of office for the president; nor does it provide for succession. From the point of view of the Baath Party, which prepared the 1970 Constitution, this seems to be appropriate since the party desired to have control over the presidency and associated the office closely with that of the Regional

Command Council's and the Revolutionary Command Council's chairman who happens to be the same person. In 1991, Saddam Hussein occupied all three positions. As prescribed by the party rules, in the case of succession, it is the vice-chairman of the RCC who succeeds the president and not the vice-president unless both offices are occupied by the same person. Thus, in the absence of a constitutional mandate, the vice-president can be appointed or dismissed at the pleasure of the president.

The president is the chief executive and the cabinet, namely the Council of Ministers, acts as the instrument of his executive authority. There is also the president's secretariat, somehow similar to the White House Staff in the United States except that it has more powers. It is called diwan; its chief has the cabinet rank, its members are special appointees which are not subject to the civil service rules established and overseen by the Public Service Council. One of the diwan's important functions is to monitor closely the Council of Ministers activities.

There are some 40 cabinet members, nearly three times the size of the U.S. cabinet, of which several are members of the Baath Party or RCC. Some of the major ministers are headed by the RCC members such as defense, foreign affairs, interior and trade. Some of the ministries unfamiliar to the American system are those of oil, irrigation, industry and minerals, planning, and religious trusts. The President presides over the cabinet where presidential policies are discussed and the means to effectuate them are determined.

The Judicial Branch

The definition of the judicial branch is quite general in the Constitution. It guarantees an independent judicial system without describing its organization and structure. The modern Iraqi court system has a traditional background which goes back to the era of the Ottoman rule, when a secular system of justice was adopted after the French model. This was later on modified by integrating into it the Islamic law. This integration was not a simple process since there were at least three dominant Islamic jurisprudences: the Shia Jafari, the Sunni Hanafi, and the Sumi Kurdish Shafir. Furthermore, other religious minorities such as Christians and Jews were allowed their religious courts with limited jurisdiction governing mainly family relations such as marriage, divorce, and inheritance.

The Constitution being silent about the organization of the judicial system and the absence of the legislative branch in the 1970s left RCC the only authority to legislate the organization and function of the judiciary. First, contrary to the Constitution that guaranteed an independent judiciary, the court system was placed under the jurisdiction of the Ministry of Justice, an arm of the executive branch. Furthermore, all judges were appointed by the president.

In 1991, the courts had jurisdiction over civil, criminal, religious, and administrative matters. The country was divided into five appellate districts each having a court of appeal located in the central cities of Baghdad, Basra, Kirkuk, Mosul, and Hillah. Below each court of appeal there were several district courts known as the courts of first instance having original jurisdiction over civil and commercial controversies. All together there were about 168 courts of the first instance. Eighteen of these which were located in the capital of the 18 provinces (governorates) were granted unlimited jurisdiction. The rest with limited jurisdiction were located in the central cities of districts, subdistricts, and governorate capitals. At the bottom were six peace courts, comparable to the small claims courts in the United States, which took care of minor litigations. Two of these were located in Baghdad and one in each of the other appellate districts. As the courts of the first instance, decisions from the peace courts could be appealed before the corresponding court of appeal.

Parallel to the civil courts, criminal cases were under the jurisdiction of the magistrates at the same sites. The decisions could be appealed from each magistrate to the corresponding sessions courts. There were six of these courts of criminal appeal. The personal status issues governed by the Islamic laws and controversies relating to management of religious endowments and trusts (wagfs) were heard and resolved in sharia (Islamic law) courts. Generally, the judges sitting in sharia courts were the same as those of the civil courts. The personal status of other religious minorities were dealt with by their own separate communal councils.

In 1977, an Administrative Court was established to decide civil litigation against the public sectors and between these sectors. At the summit of the judicial system there is the Court of Cassation, comparable to the U.S. Supreme Court, to decide the final appeals from the courts of appeals as well as the Administrative Court and, particularly, adjudicate jurisdictional conflicts between the Administrative Court and other courts. This court consists of a president (Chief Justice), vice-president, 15 or more permanent members, and a number of deputized as well as religious judges. It is divided into different sections of general, civil, criminal, administrative, and personal jurisdictions. The court of Cassation has original jurisdiction over offenses committed by high government officials.

There is also a Revolutionary Court with jurisdiction over offenses against the national security whether internal or external. This court is independent and does not come under the appellate jurisdiction of the judicial system. The proceedings are generally secret. The RCC may also, from time to time, establish special security courts with secret proceedings relating usually to matters concerned with treason, espionage and some other offenses against the state.

Regional and Local Governments

There are 18 governorates (provinces) each headed and administered by a governor appointed by the president. Each governorate or province is divided into several districts, each headed by a district officer called *gaimagam*. Each district is divided into several subdistricts each headed by a subdistrict officer called *mudir*. Each subdistrict embodies one or more municipalities each headed by a mayor. The national capital, Baghdad, has a special administrative status and its mayor, like those of other cities, is appointed by the president. There is no elective office in this administrative hierarchy of the government; all administrative heads are appointees. However, by a law enacted by RCC, since 1973 there have been popular councils on the side of each administrative subdivision with the authority to supervise, to inspect, or to criticize the administrative functions of the corresponding subdivision. But, these councils have had no policy-making or administrative authority. It appears that the council was created for the political purpose of extending and solidifying the Baath Party's popular support. There is also no evidence to show that these councils have served any significant public interest.

What may be noted from the presentation of Iraq's national, regional, and local government is that the Baath Party tightly controls the whole process of government namely, the national executive, legislative, and judicial branches, regional, and local governments. The Baath Party itself is ruled by a sole leader, Saddam Hussein, who is also the president of the country. Opposition to the Baath policies and ideals is considered antistate and ruthlessly suppressed and eliminated. There is only one elective body, the National Assembly, which, as it has been noted, has been dominated by the Baath party members and has functioned no more than being a rubber stamp for the party policies and the president's programs. When we add to this the close monitoring of the people by a well organized and rude secret police, we are witnessing an unusually harsh form of dictatorship which can rule only under a continuous suppression of the Iraqi people.

CHAPTER 4.

DEMOCRACY IN THE THIRD WORLD

Franklin D. Roosevelt once stated: "There is nothing mysterious about the foundations of our healthy and strong democracy. The basic things expected by our people of their political and economic systems are simple: equality of opportunity for youth and for others; jobs for those who can work; security for those who need it; the ending of special privileges for the few; the preservation of civil liberties for all; the enjoyment of the fruits of scientific progress in a wider and constantly rising standard of living." Much easier said than done.

The last four decades has witnessed a sincere drive by many developing countries toward democracy. But what happened to the democracies established in the 1950's, or those founded by the newly independent states of Africa in the 1960's or those crystallized in the 1970s? Within a few years many of these were either subject to military takeover or turned to authoritarianism behind the facade of democracy. Democracy, within its Western definition, has failed to establish itself as a viable and stable political system in developing societies. Our purpose in this chapter is to have a brief look at the factors affecting this instability and then, in the next chapter, looking upon the pertinent elements within the Iraqi society, we will explore the nature of a practical democracy there.

Democracy as a concept embodies two major aspects: Democracy as a process and democracy as a content or objective. The purpose of the former is the realization of the latter. Democracy as a process refers to the operation of the system for achieving democratic goals. It is based on the free and frequent elections, majority rule with minority rights, and limited governmental powers particularly in relation to individual rights.

Democracy as a content refers to the objectives that the democratic process is set to achieve. Among these are equality of opportunity from political, social, and economic viewpoints; freedom; and individualism. All these together may be classified as individual rights.[1]

The contemporary political theory is substantially distinguished from its traditional and classical form due to the fact that it extends individual rights from its purely political domain into social and economic spheres. These range from "the right to a modicum of economic welfare and security to the right to share to the full in the social heritage and to live the life of a civilized being according to the standards prevailing in the society."[2] This concept of democracy is specifically important in relation to the present conditions of developing countries where the socioeconomic issues are the most pressing and must be regarded as the prime concern of a democratic system. The paradoxical situation here is that while civil and political rights impose limitations on governmental powers, socioeconomic rights, at least in a developing society, require extended governmental actions to maintain certain standards of living, including providing for food, shelter, education, health care, and employment. Therefore, such requirement for action by the government may be detrimental to certain areas of civil rights which prohibits governmental action. However, this does not mean that the two groups of rights are incompatible.[3] These civil and socioeconomic rights are often highly interconnected because of the criterion of their importance for human well-being; and because no human rights can be regarded as absolute. The measure is the extent of immediate practibility which can affect both types of rights.[4] Actually, social and economic rights are also individual rights,[5] and civil and political rights cannot prevail if socioeconomic rights are not paid attention. The stability of the system depends on the extent of balance between the two groups of human rights. It appears that in the early stages, socioeconomic rights require more attention and as the standards of living advance the public consciousness tends toward more attention to civil rights.

One of the most complex and intractable problems in dealing with the concept of democracy is the enormous gap between the model designed for ethnically, linguistically, and culturally homogeneous nation-state and the multi-ethnic, multi-lingual, and multi-cultural societies placed within the boundaries of a nation-state mostly by the ex-colonial powers. These nation-states do not satisfy the prerequisites of the homogeneous model and thus cannot employ it successfully without modification. Iraq, Syria, Lebanon, Turkey, nearly all of the post-olonial African countries, most of the Latin American and Asian countries fall into this classification. The concept applies even to Eastern Europe as well as the ex-Soviet Union where ethnic, lingual, cultural differences has caused disintegration of the previous states and instability in the region. Among these some are considered by the Western theorists closer to democracy than the others such as Brazil, Turkey, and South Korea; some are semi democratic like Thailand and Zimbabwe, and some others such as Chile and Nigeria are attempting to relieve themselves from authoritarian regimes and move toward democracy.

Prerequisites of Democracy in Developing Societies

Democracy may mean different things for different societies based on comprehension induced and influenced by historical and cultural norms. It signifies the desirable end of many social, economic, and political pursuits under legitimatized structures.

There are factors that facilitate or obstruct democratic development. The extent of the existence of these factors in a society and their interactions determine the extent of achievable democracy. Briefly, some of these factors are as follows:

Legitimacy and Performance

In democracy, the stability depends on the consent of a majority of those governed. This consent implies that "in spite of shortcomings and failures, the existing political institutions are better than any others that might be established."[6] This legitimacy and stability depends on the one hand, on the extent of an intrinsic value commitment rooted in the political culture at all levels of society, and on the other, on the performance of the democratic system relating to the critical area of demands and needs.[7] An extended period of successful performance enhances legitimacy and enables the regime better to endure crises and challenges.[8] In the absence of a strong or sustained legitimacy the system is vulnerable to collapse in the cases of economic and social distress.[9] In less developed countries, the widespread poverty combined with the strains of modernization make it difficult for the systems that begin with low legitimacy to perform effectively, especially in the much crucial area of economy.

Democratic stability is apparently induced by consistency, prudence, and moderation in economic as well as political policies. Colombia has been an example in this regard since 1957.[10] Following the transition to democracy until recently, pragmatic economic policies produced sustained economic growth with low inflation.

In general, rapid economic growth, while accentuating problems of poverty, corruption and inequality, produces a variety of social forces for democratization such as the expansion of autonomous and more and more politically conscious, entrepreneurial and professional middle classes; the movement of labor into manufacturing; improvement in literacy, education, and communication; and the wider circulation of information and ideas. Collectively, these changes bring about political liberalization, cause increasing contact with the outside world particularly with the advanced, and industrialized democracies, and enhance the skills as well as resources for organizing autonomously to pursue the national interests.[11]

Finally, democracies have also their own negative effects. One of these is corruption which has a particularly corrosive effect on the legitimacy of the regime. Its scale and extension to the whole governmental operation, as has occurred in many countries, delegitimizes the political system as a whole. A side effect of the prevalence of political corruption is a drive for the pursuit of political power. The struggle for power replaces the debate, planning and implementation of beneficial policies and thus undermines economic development. The continuation provides grounds for justification of military takeover.

Political Leadership

Political structures and institutions are shaped by the actions and aptness of political leaders. Performance and viability, economically as well as politically, are the outcome in part of the politics and choices that political leaders make within the constraints of these structures and institutions. Poor leadership and improper choices accelerate the breakdown of democracy.[12] Among examples one may mention democratic breakdown in Turkey, South Korea, Iraq, and Brazil. Leaders dedicated to democracy reject the use of improper means for the pursuit of power and do not condone or tolerate undemocratic actions by others.[13]

Political Culture

Effective leadership rests on proper management of conflict. One of the most important factors in this regard relates to the prevailing political beliefs and values which all together form the political culture of the country. A political culture inducive to stable democracy should accommodate belief in the legitimacy of democracy, tolerance for opposing beliefs, preferences and organization; belief in compromise accompanied by moderation, pragmatism and flexibility; tendency to induce cooperation; and civility of the political process. Costa Rica[14], Venezuela[15], and Botswana[16] are suitable examples.

Socioeconomic Development

It has been argued that socioeconomic development has a fundamental effect on the way individuals and organizations relate to the political process. Advanced economic development produces greater economic security, widespread education, reduced economic inequality; it mitigates feelings of injustice and deprivation which in turn decreases the possibility of extreme political polarization.[17] It also tends to enlarge the middle class which brings about tolerance and moderation both inducive to the democratic process.[18] Sustained socioeconomic development extends political consciousness, expands political demands, and broadens political participation.[19]

A problem affecting negatively the socioeconomic development is that of rapid population growth in developing countries. As illustrated in Table 4-1, even despite improved socioeconomic conditions, population growth remains high in most of Africa, Asia and Latin America. Even if the annual growth rate is reduced to two percent as attempted by Brazil, Mexico, Turkey, Thailand and India, population will double in about 35 years. Yet the rate of population growth in most developing countries is far above two percent such as over three percent in Nigeria, Iraq, and Zimbabwe.

This rapid population growth heavily tilts the age structure toward those under the age of 15 tending to comprise 40 to 50 percent of the population.[20] From a socioeconomic viewpoint this situation substantially slows down development since this is a nonproducing dependent population to be fed, cared for, schooled and ultimately demanding employment.

From a political viewpoint, as long as the system is able to care for these newcomers, feed them, school them and find employment for them the democratic stability may not be disturbed, and eventually the population growth rates will be reduced to a manageable level of about one percent. This situation may occur first in South Korea, then in Chile and Thailand with the present population growth rates of 1.0, 1.4 and 1.5 percent respectively. In the absence of this accommodation the stability of democracy will be a question. Consequently, though political turmoil may be the result of economic mismanagement, it could also be the outcome of population explosion. All necessary and suitable measures should be applied to bring the rate of population growth under control. These measures, though often very difficult, are indispensable in order to allow the system a reasonable chance to maintain and consolidate its democracy.

State and Societal Organization

Continuation of democracy and sustaining democratic norms, require substantial limitations on governmental powers. Part of this can be achieved through legal restraints based on constitutional provisions. But the important part rests on relations between the rulers and the ruled. As to the first part, despite constitutional limitations there have been a score of leaders that have disregarded them and

Table 4-1. Development Indicators of Some Selected Third World Countries: 1965-1987

	Brazil		Mexico		Turkey		India		Thailand		Nigeria		Zimbabwe	
	1965	1987	1965	1987	1965	1987	1965	1987	1965	1987	1965	1987	1965	1987
Population in Millions, 1966 & 1987	86.5	141.4	44.9	81.9	31.9	52.6	498.8	797.5	32.0	53.6	60.0	106.6	4.5	9.0
Population Growth Rate, 1965-1980 & 1980-1987	2.4	2.2	3.1	2.2	2.5	2.3	2.3	2.1	2.9	2.0	2.5	3.4	3.1	3.7
Projected Rate of Population Growth, 1987-2000		1.8		1.9		1.9		1.8		1.5		3.0		3.0
Projected Population in Millions, 2000 & 2025	178	234	105	141	67	90	1010	1365	65	82	157	286	13	22
Current GNP per Capita in U.S. Dollars, 1966 & 1987	280	2020	490	1830	310	1210	90	300	150	850	70	370	20	580
Average Annual Growth Rate, GNP per Capita, in Percentages, 1965-1987		4.1		2.5		2.6		1.8		3.9		1.1		0.9
Average Annual Rate of Inflation, 1965-1980 & 1980-1987	31.3	166.3	13.0	68.9	20.7	37.4	7.6	7.7	6.3	2.8	13.7	10.1	6.4	12.4
Urban Population as Percentage of Total	50	75	55	71	34	47	19	27	13	21	17	33	14	26
Percentage of Labor Force in Agriculture, 1965 & 1980	49	31	50	37	75	58	73	70	82	71	72	68	79	73
Total External Public Debt as Percentage of GNP, 1970 & 1987	8.2	29.1	8.7	59.5	14.7	46.6	14.7	15.1	4.6	29.6	3.4	109.8	15.5	36.2

Sources: World Bank, *World Development Report 1983, 1987*; World Bank, *World Tables 1987*, 4th ed.; Larry Diamond Linz, Lipset, *Politics in Developing Countries*, pp. 12-13. Figures are based in current U.S. dollars and are not calculated based on the annual inflation between 1965 and 1987.

assumed authoritarian power. The limiting provisions of the constitution are respected only when the societal base is strong enough to protect them. The state must not be let to become too powerful, neither it should become too weak and unable to deliver social and economic services expected by the groups, and maintain order.

For a stable and sustained democracy there must exist a pluralistic and strongly organized civil society capable of limiting state power, stimulating political organization and citizen participation, enhancing commitment to the democratic process and values and providing different channels other than that of the state for the articulation and practice of democracy.[21] India and Costa Rica are two examples of successful and sustained democracies because of their strong and conscious civil organizations such as the press, professional associations, student groups, trade unions, business associations, and intellectuals.

Political parties are considered important supplements to these civic resources. One major problem in this regard is the ideal number of parties for stable democracy. Some argue that the two-party system is the best since it produces accommodation and moderation, each party necessarily tending to create broad political appeals.[22] However, there is a problem with the two-party system. It requires cross-cutting cleavages. If these cleavages coincide with other traditional factors such as ethnicity and religion, it might tend toward polarization of conflicts thus producing civil strifes and breakdown of democracy.[23]

Some others have argued that the multiparty system is more appropriate if it remains moderate and does not become polarized.[24] The more appropriate system for democratic stability appears to be a representational multi-party system with strong linkages to distinct social groups, broad social and ideological bases, committed to facilitating the involvement of potentially disaffected groups in legitimate political process and with extremist parties unable to attract significant attention.[25] The consolidation of a reasonably stable and workable party system is necessary for a stable and sustained democracy at least at its early stages. The main problem with a political party system is a tendency toward gaining power and centralizing authority. Any political party reaching this stage of power may become in itself a significant burden on the democratic process. The best way toward democracy seems to be through highly decentralized voluntary local associations. This eliminates to a great degree the power politics embodied in political party system. This is a system used in the Iranian political process since the abolition of political parties in June, 1987. In an advanced stage of democracy which occurs in a highly technological society, political parties becoming a burden upon the democratic process will effectively disappear.[26]

Ethnic and Regional Disparity

In any society where there are major territorially based ethnic or regional cleavages, there must be provision for devolution and decentralization of power. The absence of such arrangements will bring about insecurity inducive to violent conflict and even secessionalism. The examples include Lebanon, Iraq, Yugoslavia, and Czechoslovakia.

The problem can be resolved by instituting federalism, autonomy, statehood or other politically decentralized system. The absence of such accommodations can lead to forced imposition of central authority and deterioration of democracy. When the regime responds to the demands of this mobilized ethnic group by exclusion and repression, violence festers inducive to military intervention and takeover of the system.

But none of these decentralization arrangements may be sufficient to maintain democracy if the new structure is not balanced as far as the sharing of power is concerned. The failure of the First Nigerian Republic in the 1960s, and its subsequent civil war, was because of the gross imbalance of the three-region federal system resulting in political hegemony of one group. The situation had to be rectified finally by forming a 19-state federal system, the Second Republic. It gave Nigeria's many ethnic groups a much greater sense of political security and autonomy.

Foreign Influence

While political development and changes are primarily internal and are considered domestic affairs, it must be recognized the manner by which these structures have been affected and shaped historically by a variety of foreign factors such as colonial rule, cultural infiltration, and demonstration effects.[27] There are numerous past and present examples of Western and U.S. support for authoritarian regimes and actual attempts towards undermining or even overthrowing popularly elected governments that appeared threatening their interests;[28] Chile in the 1970s, Nicaragua and Granada in the 1980s. At the same time, many of the now-established democracies were imposed by foreign powers through armed conquest or colonization,[29] Philippines and Panama are two examples.

The most important foreign influences on the prospects for democracy seem to be in the area of economy. There are enormous international economic constraints that may cause severe limits on the maneuverability and impair the legitimacy of democratic systems. Among these obstacles are severe indebtedness, obstracted export markets, and steep balance of payments crises.

In general the consolidation of democracy may proceed for a time in the face of somehow weak economic performance and sharply diminishing belief in the effectiveness of the system, Spain being an example. However, the new democracies of the developing countries are deeply in trouble by economic crises. The relief from this situation, at least in part, depends on a variety of factors in international economic system over which they have little influence if any.

After enumerating all these problems and situations facing developing countries in their attempts to establish a stable and sustained democracy it is easy to assume that consolidating democracy in such a setting requires skillful political crafting, wise policy choices, and determination by the leadership to carry them out. These tough decisions must be directed first regarding the structures and then toward resolving economic conditions such as narrowing down the enormous inequalities between rich and poor, gradually reducing the state ownership and control of the means of production and distribution, and attracting foreign investment.

Giving prime attention to the structures requires forming the kind of system which will respond to social, regional, and ethnic situations and will minimize conflicts detrimental to the democratic process. It is only under such political structures with major groups consensus that the leadership can take steps to improve socioeconomic conditions. Since the cultural and historical factors differ, often substantially, from one society to another, the political structure and process must also be different in order to accommodate the existing dominant norms and factors. Accordingly, there cannot be a single model employable by all or most of the developing countries. The most that can be suggested is to take under consideration all the factors discussed in this chapter and attempt to crystalize a form of democracy most suitable for the country and do not hesitate to revise and restructure it toward attaining a more suitable and durable democratic regime. There is no need to stress that a durable democracy is possible only in a politically conscious society which materializes through education. A politically educated electorate is a prerequisite for democracy.

Democratic Authoritarianism

There is another political theory relating to developing countries that has been sustained as more suitable, more effective, and more beneficial.[30]

This system is based on the concept that the economic problems of the society must receive prime attention and priority over any other development. The theory is that movement toward economic democracy will eventually lead toward gaining of individual freedoms and development of political democracy as a consequence. The theory emphasizes that freedom cannot be achieved without bread. Sustained economic development under an authoritarian system reduces the existing economic inequality, produces a feeling of economic security, causes widespread education leading toward increased political consciousness. It also mitigates feelings of injustice and deprivation and thus decreasing the possibility of extreme political polarization.

Yet the system is not fully authoritarian but certain fundamental institutions of democracy are created and democratic processes are instituted to stimulate popular support for and participation in economic development programs.

This is a kind of mixture of democracy and authoritarianism primarily sustained and employed by Lee Kuan Yew, the prime minister of Singapore from 1959 to 1990. Because of its enormous success in socioeconomic development, it is a system most talked about among southeast Asian countries.

Intellectual and iron fisted, Lee Kuan Yew is apotheosis of enlightened autocracy. He is actually a despot who placed his people's interests ahead of his own and avoided the temptation of financial enrichment.[31] As prime minister, he defined and practiced the "highest form of Asian-style democracy," transforming a colonial port into one of the most highly controlled, yet best governed, city-states in the world.

Central to this concept is that economic development must precede political liberalization. He argues that the countries of the Pacific Rim are booming precisely because they are more advanced economically than politically and not in spite of it. He considers a virtue what Western analysts see as imbalance.[32]

His concept is based on the Confucian philosophy of Eastern Asia, a belief that has influenced China's political thought since the 19th century, Korea's since the 15th, and Japan's for about three centuries. The rest of the region is also influenced, in different degrees, by the Confucian thought; among these are Hong Kong, Taiwan, Singapore, Thailand, Indonesia, Malaysia, and Philippines. The philosophy stresses a rational natural order, of which man is a harmonious element, and a social order based on strict ethical rules and centering on a unified state governed by men of education and superior ethical wisdom. It fosters consensus.[33]

According to this philosophy, as Lee puts it, "The minority recognize they are the minority and go along with the majority for the time being, which lessens the contention." While Lee does not reject the West, he argues that it is unrealistic to expect Asians and Americans to behave the same way politically, given the vast cultural differences that separate the two. Asians, in general, are brought up respecting authority, valuing consensus. Deference toward authority is deeply imbedded in their culture and a very high value is placed on order. Thus the concept of a "loyal opposition", central to the debates in Western democracies, is not accepted by many Asian leaders. Confucianism teaches that leaders are by definition virtuous; accordingly, political opponents are considered enemies.

These cultural forces are in action in Singapore. Lee Kuan Yew's regime's Internal Security Act allows detention without trial, control of the mass media, and close regulation of virtually every aspect of life. However, there is no doubt that people want Lee's People's Action Party (PAP) to run the country.

There was even concern that the opposition, in 1991's scrupulously honest parliamentary elections, won four out of 81 seats. Many

Singaporians draw distinction between freedom and liberty. They get fined $125 for driving without a seat belt, but they can walk the streets without fear, breathe clean air, and they can vote.

There is no political stagnation in the region as a whole. Recently, South Koreans rejected the ruling Democratic Liberal Party; Taiwan is to hold its first free and full legislative elections in four decades at the end of the year. Filipinos ventured to the polls and chose their first honestly elected president in 23 years. Thais took to the streets to throw out a prime minister who had not been elected. Even in Indonesia, the ruling party has just repealed a decree that gave President Suharto sweeping powers to run the country. As argued, this move was consistent with the country's evolution toward democracy which is considered a moving point on a spectrum and not a rigid ideology.[35]

Iran is another example of this mixed system comparable to that of Singapore. Here the Islamic norms replaces Confucianism. Intellectual, experienced, and determined, President Hashemi Rafsanjani, like Lee Kuan Yew, has placed his people's interests ahead of his own without the temptation of self-enrichment. He has defined and practiced the highest form of "Islamic democracy" intently directing his country of nearly 70 million, devastated as a result of eight years of war, toward social, economic and political development.

Like Lee, his emphasis is on economic development. He knows that the strength and prosperity of his people depend on the level of economic advancement. His concept of government is based on the Islamic prescriptions which stresses a rational living order in which the individual is a harmonious element as inseparable part of the universe and the operatoin of society is based on strict ethical rules prescribed by Allah, the Creator, conveyed through his Messenger Mohammad. The state is governed, according to the Islamic tradition based on the teachings of Mohammad, with men of wisdom, high ethics and education consented to by the people.

In order to ascertain the success of the development programs debated and approved by the majority of the people's representatives, no fundamental opposition is accepted. To sustain the efficiency and effectiveness of the development programs the contention must be reduced. Thus, the opposing minority need to go along with the majority for the time being. It should not attempt to hamper the programs and create obstacles for development. The chosen leaders, being scholars in Islam and strict practitioners of the religion, are necessarily virtuous leaving no ground for opposition. The political process in Iran is quite dynamic and there is no political stagnation. In recent parliamentary elections, the people ousted most of the radical fundamentalists from their legislative body, the Majlis. The rebellious Majlis (parliament) dominated by the late Imam Khomeini's hardline followers had become the last obstacle standing in the way of President Rafsanjani's socioeconomic reforms. After his election as president in August 1989, he set up a cabinet wholly loyal to him consisting of handpicked technocrats, among them were many non-political Western-trained executives. Rafsanjani, solidly backed by Iman Khomenei, will have now more elbow-room for carrying out his project primarily concerned with reconstruction of the economy and opening Iran to the world outside. Rid of the most vocal of his radical opponents, he has now prepared the ground for carrying out his programs.

However, the Third Majlis, while ultimately did not seriously hamper Rafsanjani's projects, was a safety valve through which the people voiced their discontent with the administration. This is now likely to be expressed in the streets. At the same time a substantial part of the people, hit by the constantly rising cost of living, believes that if the head of the state is let to carry out his programs he will finally bring prosperity back to the country.[37] The recent elections saw also the impressive advancement of women in Iranian politics. Their representation increased from only four in the Third Mijlis to 22 in the present parliament. Presently, women constitute 18 percent of the work force and 43 percent of the university students. While seriously concerned with socioeconomic development, Rafsanjani also has been seeking how best to cope with the reality of Western power, how to beat it, how to use it, and how to incorporate what is useful without losing the essence of the national culture.[38] Education being an essential element for social, economic and political development has become one of the primary concerns of the government. It is strongly encouraged at every level, and educational institutions and facilities are rapidly expanding.

Mexico also may be considered within this category. It has been ruled in an authoritarian manner by one party (PRI) for many decades yet with substantial economic successes. Now that economic conditions have improved the organized opposition has been increasing and the ruling party finds itself in trouble.[39] This is also an example of Lee Kuan Yew's belief that economic development brings about political liberalization.

In all these examples of authoritarian-democratic regimes, the operation of the system is primarily focused on the socioeconomic development which ultimately opens the door for other freedoms and democratic norms.

To achieve democracy, either of the two approaches faces a rough road to ride through; it requires considerable patience and forbearance from the part of government, interest groups, and the public as a whole. The success also depends on the intentions and policies of the major industrialized democracies in dealing with critical issues of development in the developing country such as external debt, trade, and technology transfer. Friendly response to international policies and interests of these political and economic giants is also essential in order to provide opportunities for political and economic support toward development. For example, in this regard Iran is facing formidable obstraction by the United States in its economic, trade and technological relations with other nations.

CHAPTER 5.

AN ANALYSIS TOWARD SOLUTION: A MODIFIED SYSTEM

Taking into consideration the obstacles to and possibilities of democracy in developing countries as analyzed above, we now are in a proper position to take a constructive look at Iraq's conditions within this context and attempt to lay a general ground for democracy in this country.

Legitimacy and Performance

In any kind of democracy, even under democratic-authoritarian system, the stability depends on the consent of a majority of the population. Thus a periodic reference to the public for the approval of institutional legitimacy becomes an indispensable part of the governing a nation in any form of democracy. For example, in early 1970s the people of Chile, through an honest and clean electoral process, chose Marxism as an appropriate system for the development and prosperity in their country. Since a Marxist system was not an acceptable form of government for the United States particularly when it was chosen democratically, it had to be destroyed by any possible means. As stated above, the consent of giant economic powers, especially a superpower like the United States was essential for the survival of the democratic system chosen by the people of a less developed society. Thus the government of Chile headed by Dr. Allende, a Marxist, was placed under economic pressure and finally, through the efforts of the U.S. Central Intelligence Agency, was overthrown by the military and replaced by a destructive and suppressive military dictatorship. Accordingly, the question of legitimacy must first be accepted by the people of the country and also be acceptable to the major powers having political and economic interest in the region.

In the case of Iraq, the Western world's interest in oil is a dominant and powerful factor. European countries and the United States in particular must be made sure in having easy and secure access to oil reserves in the Middle East. Iraq is the holder of such reserves and is a neighbor to other countries with immense oil reserves such as Saudi Arabia, Kuwait, Iran, and the United Emirates. In the case of Iraq, first, the free flow of its oil must be guaranteed by the kind of system that rules the country, and second, such a system must not be a threat to free flow of oil from the neighboring countries.

Except for the 1979 revolution in Iran, Iraq was the first oil-producing country in the Middle East to face a far reaching political revolution. However, unlike Iran the legacy of the revolution in Iraq today appears very ambiguous. Socialism as the foundation of Baath ideology was clearly in opposition to the conservative autocratic regimes of the neighboring Persian Gulf states and expressedly against capitalism. Yet, in practice, the Baath aligned itself with those countries whose regimes it despised as well as with the capitalist industrialized West.

Conciliation between these two approaches, namely ideological commitment to socialism and close relationship with antisocialist regimes, was very difficult and its justification highly questionable by many including a large sector of the prosocialist intellectuals in Iraq.

The slightest opposition was harshly punished. When, in June 1979, Saddam Hussein became president, President Ahmad Hassan Al-Bakr was stripped of all his positions and placed under house arrest. Immediately following this event there was a massive purge of the Baath Regional Command Council (RCC) Muhyi Rashid, its secretary was forced to confess and shot along with his whole family. Some one-third of the RCC members, many outstanding ideologues, were executed. The purge continued into the top-ranking party members and some 500 were executed. Several months later (August, 1980) Mohammad Bagir al-Sadr and his sister Bint al-Huda, both being symbols of the Iraqi Shias opposition, were executed. This was the way the initial undisputed authority of President Saddam Hussein was established at the cost of the bloody elimination of irreplaceable brilliant Iraqi leaders and thinkers.

The secret police was the right arm of the President for control of the population. Baghdad was divided into security zones each with a headquarter as a surveillance center hooked to video cameras hidden on roof tops, built into statues and other public monuments on the squares and streets. They covered intersections, the major streets and surroundings, creating a comprehensive network of surveillance for each zone. Though cameras are sold in Iraq, but taking pictures in public places requires the written authorization of the Ministry of Interior, otherwise the person taking pictures would be a suspect. Simply, the secret police is all-pervasive ruler in Iraq.[1]

Another instrument of terror and control has been the Military Intelligence (Estikhbarat) which imposes control over actions against Iraqi residents abroad. In this respect it employs embassy personnel. It operates also as a surveillance device within the armed forces. The extent of the authority of this organization can be comprehended by Saddam Hussein's speech in February of 1980 in which he stated that "the hand of the revolution can reach out to its enemies wherever they are found." It has been considered the instrument of assassination of quite few Iraqi opposition and other leaders abroad.[2]

Concerning the internal security, suspects do not have to do anything to be victimized. The secret police in Iraq invents their enemies. Justification for this authority was granted by Saddam Hussein in his 1978 speech:

> The revolution chooses its enemies, and we say chooses its enemies because some enemies are chosen by it from among the people who run up against its program and intend to harm it. The revolution chooses as enemies those people who intend to deviate it from its main principles and starting points.[3]

There is also the party militia created by the Baath Party which remains an extremely important component of the Baathist ideology as a counterbalance to the army. Its strength has been estimated between 170,000 to 250.000.

Today the authoritative violence is the instrument of control. No one dares to oppose authority; fear dominates. Sinister and impenetrable forces operate on helpless population under the assumed rationality of the Revolution. Cruel institutional practices in Iraq such as confession rituals, executions, corpse displays, public hangings, and tortures, are designed to install and maintain fear. These also are presented as the state's right to confront and eliminate the nation's enemies. To dramatize public fear, often everything is secret, from the arrest, charges, interrogation, extraction of evidence, the trial and judgment as well as execution of the sentence. It creates an atmosphere of horror by the knowledge of inevitability of anonymous torture and death under any condition. Therefore, in Iraq, legitimacy is not established by the consent of the people but it is imposed by force, dictatorial and brutal authority. Any voice with the slightest contradiction is savagely silenced.

A Future Perspective: The United Republics of Iraq

After a brief introduction to the historical background of Iraq and its present government, cultural and political conditions, we now attempt to take a look to the future of the country from a democratic perspective.

A true definition of democracy involves the whole societal system from political, economic, and social standpoints. Socioeconomic democracy is the most important aspect of democracy and the most desired in less developed countries and yet the most difficult to achieve. The Baath government tried to achieve it at least partially.

In the absence of political democracy, achieving socioeconomic democracy has to be forced upon the people at the cost of individual freedom. This process was tried in Iraq at a tremendous cost in human life, suppression, and waste of precious resources which were directed toward building up a military power rather than using it for socioeconomic development.

The unjustified ambitions of the sole ruler and the military since 1979 have cost the Iraqi people two devastating wars. They have caused the destruction of the societal infrastructure and communities, the loss of over a half million lives, extended poverty, continuing loss of lives, particularly, those of children, spread of disease, and the shortage of the necessities for continuation of a normal life. All of these have been the results of these two wars. Worse yet, the future resources of Iraq are mortgaged to the payments of nearly 200 billion dollars for damages brought upon Iran and Kuwait.

The sorrowful experiences of the past 12 years emphatically prescribe the need for some kind of stable and durable political democracy. As presented in the previous chapter, some believe that socioeconomic development in less developed countries can be achieved better and faster under benevolent dictatorship. Yet it is clear that no meaningful development can be attained without people's approval and active participation. Benevolent dictatorship will also necessarily put value on the lives of its citizens, allow discussion of the issues, protect human lives rather than destroying them by thousands at will.

We must disagree with any kind of dictatorship no matter how benevolent. This is the age of enlightenment with worldwide electronic information-communication systems. Less developed nations are exposed to what is going on in the rest of the world. Inspiration, drive, and desire for democratic way of life has exploded in the Eastern European countries and has caused disintegration of the Soviet Union into many independent countries. Islamic fundamentalism has established its own version of democracy in Iran; it is also rampant in Algeria, Sudan and several other countries. Even China, the only major bastion of Leninism-Marxism is being obliged to ease its grip in certain areas of socioeconomic life. In this regard one must make a clear distinction between a benevolent dictatorship and a disciplined and responsible democracy. The latter is definitely more suitable to the conditions of less developed countries.

Democracy is also going through different stages of change among developed countries. The Western European countries are in a delicate process of economic and political integration. The native Canadians as well as the French speaking Quebec are driving for more autonomy. Democracy perhaps is in more trouble in the United States than in any other developed country. While Americans do care about democracy, they feel politically impotent. Negative campaigning, controlling effect of money, unattended promises are causing Americans to turn away from politics and elections. Only about 50 percent of eligible Americans vote in presidential elections, 35 to 40 percent in congressional elections, and 20-25 percent in local elections.[4] So, the present government in the United States from top to bottom is a government of the minority rather than that of the majority of the eligible voters. Americans feel cut off from most policy issues; they feel these policies do not reflect their concerns nor have connection to them.[5] Americans feel they are heard only when in large groups they angrily protest policy decisions. They feel to have lost their place in politics.   The electronic information-communication system is controlled by whomever can pay for it. There is no ongoing direct relationship and give-and-take between public officials and citizens; Americans want their concerns understood and decisions explained to them. Americans are waiting for political excitements, bringing to life their dormant civic duty with opportunity to cause fundamental changes necessary to enliven the undermined democratic process.

Struggle for democracy has become universal affecting even the harsh tribal dictatorships in Saudi Arabia and Kuwait. Iraq is not going to remain immune from these winds of change. The trend is toward a system of government which is based on the voice and will of the people rather than on the will of one person or a small group of leaders.

Our efforts here are to propose the foundation for such a democratic system in Iraq based on its sociopolitical conditions. Some parts from our suggestions may seem utopian considering the present conditions of the country but the Constitution is the fundamental law of the society and is formulated not only to accommodate the present conditions but embody principles that are of permanent nature in democracy. These principles may not have sufficiently supportive grounds to be effectuated now but they are of permanent guidance in gradual progress toward a meaningful democratic society. A good example in this regard is the Bill of Rights in the United States Constitution (the first ten amendments to the Constitution) which was ratified as part of the Constitution in the late 18th century but it did not become functionally effective until early in the 20th century, some 150 years later. It started with freedom of speech and press of the First Amendment applying to the states in 1925. The founders considered it imperative to place these fundamental human rights in the United States Constitution regardless of the impossibility of their application at the time. Today, nearly all the rights embodied in the Bill of Rights are strongly sustained and applied in all national and state levels.

For the purpose of establishing a democratic society, the new constitution of Iraq will have the following features: question of territorial and political structure, question of basic governmental structure and representation, and question of individual rights. Toward achieving this purpose it will be useful to review the Iraqi Interim Constitution of 1970 which is mostly in effect today. This review will help us in determining which parts of this constitution will be sustained and which parts need modification or a complete change to give Iraqi people a workable democratic system where all the major religious and ethnic groups will have appropriate share in their political as well as socioeconomic life.

Representation and Political Structure

The question of representation is the most significant and at the same time the most complex ingredient of the democratic process in Iraq. There are sharp ethnic differences and historical contradictions which cannot be resolved unless there is first a sincere initial desire for compromise among the leaders of different groups based on the realities of life in the country, and then, there is a sustained direction toward bringing about a sense of consciousness for self-direction and self-realization among the different groups in the country. A sense of cooperativeness for national progress is essential.

One strong element to be considered is the religion. In general, this has created three major groups. The Shia Muslim Arabs consisting of some 55 percent of the population concentrated in the lower half of the country as presented in the map (Figure 5-1). Sunni Muslim Arabs consisting of about 20 percent residing mostly in the central and western part of the territory; and the Sunni Kurds, about 25 percent of the population occupying the northern part of the country.

There are no definite dividing lines between these three major Islamic groups but large overlapping areas. The map on Figure 5-1 illustrates the situation.

Figure 5-1. Ethnic and Religious Distribution, 1988

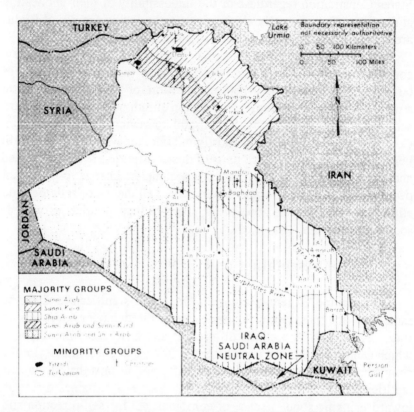

Source: Helen Chapin Metz, *Iraq: A Country Study,* Federal Research Division, Library of Congress, 1990, P. 82.

One of the most undemocratic policies in Iraq has been the control of the government by the minority Sunni Arabs to the detriment of proper participation by the Kurds and particularly by the Shias which constitute the majority of the population. Any stable system will require proper representation and participation of all these groups in governmental process.

At the same time there is a tendency toward a certain desirable degree of autonomy by both the Kurds and Shias. Such desire is much stronger from the part of the Kurds since they do not consider themselves Arabs and are of Persian stock. Therefore, the new system

Figure 5-2. Federalism, Formula One

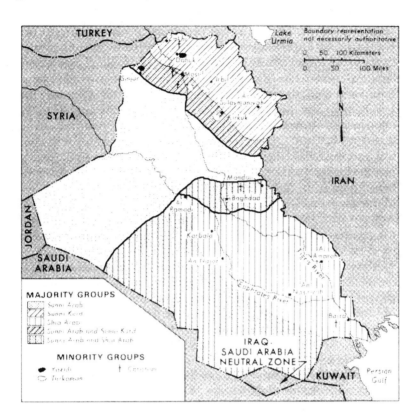

of government in Iraq must accommodate all these differences and past inequalities.

The desire toward autonomy can be resolved by the creation of a suitable federal system. Territorially there are alternative forms to this federalism.

First, to divide Iraq into four regions as presented in Figure 5-2, each having its own autonomous system, and the national government centered in Baghdad, the national capital. This appears to be the most simple way. Except the central region where the capital of the nation, Baghdad, is located, the other three states each will be predominantly populated by one of the three major groups. The northern state will be Kurdish, the western one Sunni Arab, and the southern one Shia

Arab. The central region will not have much ethnic problems since all three groups are nearly proportionally present there. Baghdad will be the national territory where all the central offices of the national government will be located having its branches within the states necessary for the expansion of national services to the residents of the states.

This system of federalism has one major problem. The area within each state where there is an overlapping minority population from the neighboring religious and ethnic groups will be under control of the majority. This will make a minority from one group subject to domination by another. Considering the historical evidences since independence, this situation more likely will create instability, opposition, perhaps resulting in certain kinds of suppression if the majority rule governs within the state without regard to minority rights. As presented in Figure 5-1, there are two major areas where members of two groups live together. One is between the Kurdish section and the Sunni Arab area. The other, comprises a much larger area in the southwest where Sunni Arabs and Shias live together.

This brings us to a second proposal of federalism. Here, as presented in Figure 5-3 the country is divided into five autonomous states and a central territory. State A is predominantly Kurd and will be ruled by the Kurds; State B is a mixture of the Kurds and Sunni Arabs, where the power necessarily will be shared by both; State C will be predominantly Sunni Arab and will be ruled by them; State D will be a mixture of Sunni Arabs and Shia Arabs and the power will be shared by them; and State E will be predominently Shia Arab and will be ruled by them. In the central territory, all three groups proportionally will share the power. The national government will be stationed in Baghdad and will exercise its constitutional powers from there extending over all the territory. The extent of the state and national powers will be determined by the National Constitution.

From a practical viewpoint, none of these two systems is probable since it requires a total transformation of the present subdivisions into new ones. It will also cause a substantial differentiation in political power as well as economic resources.

The third and more pragmatic way of creating a federal system will be to keep the present 18 regional governorates and attempt to build a federal system which will tend to resolve the ethnic and religious problems, will divide economic resources equitably, and equalize

Figure 5-3. Federalism, Formula Two

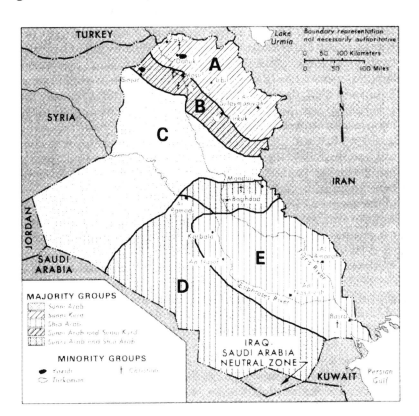

political power. Considering all these aspects, the nation will be divided into six states and a national territory as presented in Figure 5-4.

Except Kurdistan (State A) in the north, the other states are presented by a capital letter. The appropriate name for each state has to be determined later on by the National Constitutional Convention.

The six states are created as follows: State A to include the three districts (the title of governorate is changed to district) of D'hok, Arbil, and Sulaymaniyah with a total population of 1,979,000 and the territorial expansion of 36,347 square kilometers. This state will be predominantly Kurdish. Its creation will accomplish the centuries old

Figure 5-4. Federalism, Formula Three

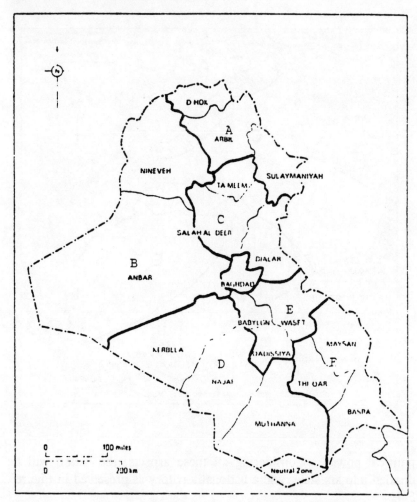

desire of the Kurdish people for having an autonomous state of their own.

State B will consist of the two districts of Nineweh and Anbar with a total population of 2,325,000 and the territorial area of 175,421 square kilometers. This state will be predominantly Sunni Arab with a small minority of Kurds in the north and Shias in the south.

State C, comprising of the districts of Tameen, Salah ad Deen, and Diyala, will have a population of 2,217,000 and a territory of 58,687 kilometers.[2] This state will have nearly equal population of Kurdish, concentrated in the north, Shias mostly in the south, and Sunni Arabs mostly in the central part.   There will not be a single dominant majority group and thus the government will be shared by all three major groups.

State D, consisting of the districts of Kerbala, Najaf, and Muthanna will have a population of 1,492,000 and the territorial area of 83,962 square kilometers. The population will be a mixture of Sunni Arabs and Shias and the government will be shared between the two major groups.

State E, formed by the districts of Babylon, Waset, and Quadissiya will have a population of 2,130,000 with an area of 31,073 square kilometers.

State F, comprising of the districts of Maysan, Thi-Qar, and Basra with a population of 2,290,000 will occupy a territory of 47,799 square kilometers. Both states will be predominantly Shia and ruled by the Shia Arabs.

The District of Baghdad with a population of 3,845,000 and a territory of 5,159 square kilometers will constitute the national territory and the seat of the national government.   The branches of certain national offices, as allowed by the constitution, will extend into the states to perform national functions.

Population Distribution

Table 5-1 presents the areas and population of all the territories. Table 5-2 presents the urban and rural population in each district within each state as well as the total state population. One beneficial aspect of this subdivision is the ratio of population distribution between the new states. Except for the State D which embodies a large scarcely populated desert area, the population of the other five states varies between 2 and 2.3 million. The urban population varies between 1.2 and 1.5 million and the rural, between 0.77 and 0.88 million. These demonstrate a close population distribution among the five states. More interestingly, their urban and rural populations are also comparable. Thus, there is a near equal distribution of manpower

Table 5-1. Areas and Population Density, 1987

State Departments	Land area (km²)	Population (1000s)	Density (per km²)
A	36,374	1,979	54.4
Kurdistan			
B	175,421	2,325	13.3
C	58,687	2,217	37.7
D	83,962	1,492	17.8
E	31,073	2,130	68.5
F	47,799	2,290	47.9
Bagdad	5,159	3,845	745.3

Calculated from different sources: the figures are approximations and may not be exact.

Table 5-2. Urban and Rural Population in Each State, 1987 (in thousands)

State	District	Urban	Rural	Total
	Dahuk	160	133	293
Kurdustan	Arbil	475	268	743
(A)	Sulaymaniyah	543	400	943
	Total	1178	801	1979
(B)	Nineveh	982	525	1507
	Anbar	538	280	818
	Total	1520	805	2325
(C)	Tamin	473	120	593
	Saiah ad Deen	400	324	724
	Diyala	465	435	900
	Total	1338	879	2217
(D)	Karbala	341	115	456
	Najaf	568	155	723
	Muthanna	163	150	313
	Total	1072	420	1492
(E)	Qadissiya	321	240	561
	Wasit	260	200	460
	Babylon	669	440	1109
	Total	1250	880	2130
(F)	Maysan	275	225	500
	DhiQar	468	450	918
	Basra	782	90	872
	Total	1525	765	2290
Baghdad	Baghdad	3600	245	3845
(G)				
	Total Pop. (est.)			16728

among the states. In the case of the state D except for the large unproductive desert area the manpower for the rest of the state will be comparable to those of the other states. While its rural population is about 50 percent of the other states, its urban population is equal to 91 percent of Kurdistan which is the lowest among the five states and 79 percent of the average urban population among all of the five states. Therefore, this form of subdivision of the country into six states provides for an equitable distribution of manpower and human resources.

Distribution of Major Economic Resources

The purpose here is not a detailed and exact study of the economic resources of the six states. It is an overview of the situation for the purpose of a rough estimation of the major resources, such as oil, agriculture, and manpower. The purpose is whether or not the subdivision of the country into these six states could be sustained as justifiable from an economic viewpoint; whether or not these states can be self sustaining economically.

Table 5-3 below shows that wheat and barley are the two major agricultural productions in Iraq. The area under wheat production averaged about 5 million mesharra or about 3.125 million acres. Barley production covered an area of about 3 million mesharra or approximately 1.875 million acres. Figure 5-5 demonstrates yield per hectar (2.5 acres) of land of the three major crops; and the total amount produced annually from 1955 to 1984.

A look at the production of these two major crops within the six states reveals that their production in all the states except those of the two states of D and F are near evenly distributed. The production in F is about one-third of the others and in D is almost negligible. Figure 5-6 presents this situation.

However, the shortcoming of agricultural production in F is offset by its oil resources. The three states of A, B, and C also have oil resources and will benefit from its income. Figure 5-7 illustrates the oil resources of Iraq.

Oil is the source of major wealth of the country. Figure 5-8 shows that Iraq did benefit greatly from the international oil price increase in the 1970s. The figure shows a sudden collapse in production and

Table 5-3. Major Crops - Areas Under Cultivation in Iraq

	1976	1977	1978	1979
		(100 mesharra)		
Cereals				
Wheat	59,972	34,304	59,826	43,112
Barley	23,028	21,435	28,573	30,412
Rice	2,096	2,539	2,189	2,348
Industrial crops				
Cotton	1,013	837	685	610
Tobacco	339	500	469	388
Linseed	36	39	35	114
Sesame	480	367	723	533
Sugar cane	120	130	169	169
Sunflower	320	327	180	513
Vegetables				
Dry onion	389	421	409	328
Dry broad beans	633	582	588	324
Chick peas	547	598	575	725
Okra	399	461	498	548
Tomato	1,825	1,625	1,613	1,145
Broad beans, green	723	695	560	535
Watermelons	1,791	1,826	1,782	1,372
Cucumber	577	790	799	980

(Note: 1 mesharra equals 0.25 ha)

Source: Central Statistical Organization, Annual Abstract of Statistics 1979, Baghdad. From Peter Beaumont, G. Blake, and J. Wagstaff, *The Middle East: A Geographical Study*, 2nd Ed. (New York: Halsted Press, 1988), p. 352.

Figure 5-5. Variations in annual production and yields for wheat, barley and rice in Iraq, 1955-1984

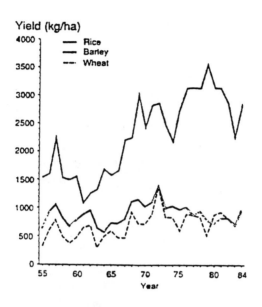

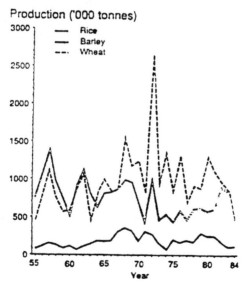

Source: Peter Beaumont, G. Blake, and J. Wagstaff, *The Middle East: A Geographical Study*, 2nd ed. (New York: Halsted Press, 1988) p. 354.

Figure 5-6. Wheat and barley production in the major administrative units of Iraq in 1979.

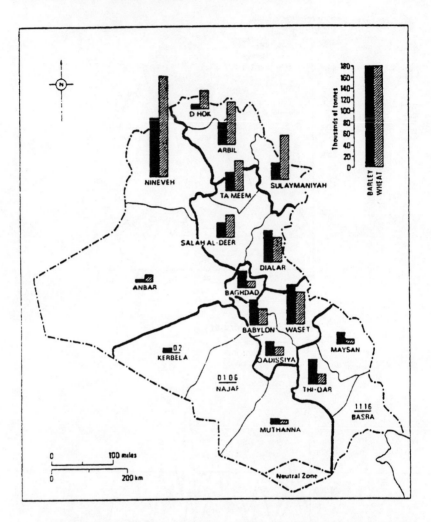

Source: Peter Beaumont, G. Blake, and J. Wagstaff, *The Middle East: A Geographical Study*, 2nd ed. (New York: Halsted Press, 1988) p. 353.

Figure 5-7. Oil Resources of Iraq, Iran, Kuwait, and Saudi Arabia

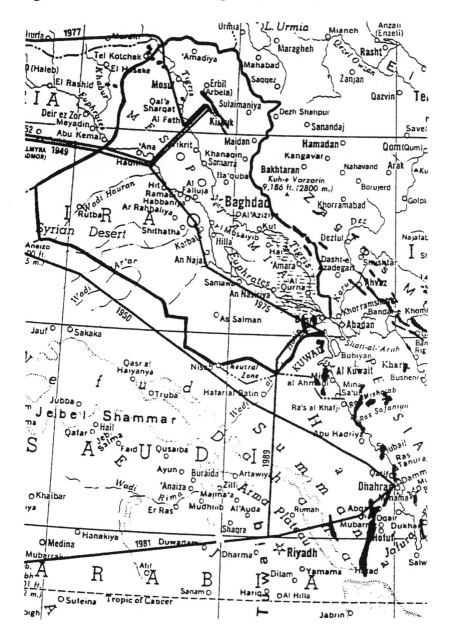

corresponding revenues since 1980 because of the war with Iran and restrictions imposed on the export of oil. Presently, a near total prohibition is imposed by the U.N. Security Council on the sale of oil. More likely, for years a substantial part of revenues from the production of oil will be allocated to pay for war damages to Kuwait and Iran which in both cases Iraq has been found to be the aggressor. The extent of the annual payment for war damages is estimated to be limited to around 30 percent of the total sale of oil. This being true, Iraq will still have access to 70 percent of revenues from the oil. The manner by which the oil revenues will be divided between the state owning the resources and the national government will be determined by the Constitution. This could be determined based on the experiences by the other countries such as Colombia where 40 percent of the revenues go to the regional and local governments and 60 percent to the national government. The only state incapable of economic survival in par with the other five is state D. However, it must be noted that the two cities of Kerbala and Najaf are the most holy and sacred cities to Shia Muslims and hundreds of thousands of pilgrims from other Shia territories including Iran and Afghanistan and all the areas within Iraq continually visit these cities and spend money there. There are no statistics about the amount of revenues from this source. It certainly could amount to a substantial figure.

From the economic viewpoint it may be advisable to distribute this state among the three neighboring states of B, E, and F, allocating Muthanna to F, Najaf to E and Kerbala to B, and thus divide the country into only five states. But this will disturb the religious and ethnic equilibrium which was the main purpose of creating a federal system. Shias in the district of Kerbala will fall under the domain of the state B governed by Sunni Arabs. On the other hand, Sunni Arabs in districts of Najaf and Muthanna will fall under the domain of the two states of E and F governed by Shias.

The best alternative for the purpose of stability and democracy is to keep the state of D and stablize its economy through national grants and other means. This will require a general consent by the other five states to share a small part from their incomes through national channels with their less fortunate partner. Since the population of D is a mixture of Shia and Sunni Arabs, both Sunni and Shia states will have no strong objections toward national economic assistance to this state. As it will be seen, the new national constitution provides for such provisions of equalization through the equitable distribution of the national wealth.

Figure 5-8. Oil Production and Oil Revenues

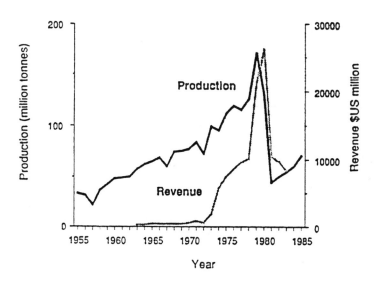

Source: Peter Beaumont, G. Blake, and J. Wagstaff, *The Middle East: A Geographical Study*, 2nd ed. (New York: Halsted Press, 1988) p. 350.

Labor and Manpower

The total population of Iraq in 1987 was calculated at 16,278,000. The annual population growth is over three percent, one of the highest in the world. Table 5-4 demonstrates that in 1985 Iraq had the highest population growth rate of 3.6 percent in the Middle East. Of the total population 45.7 percent were under the age of 15 or nonproductive consumers.

On the other hand, Figure 5-9 shows that a very small percentage of the population was of old and nonproductive age of 65 and over, amounting to only about four percent of the population. This leaves nearly 50 percent of the population within the productive labor force.

Of this, nearly two million are between the ages of 15-19. Though this is the high school age, nearly one half of Iraqis at this age level are part of the work force.

As it has been presented before, this work force is quite evenly divided among the states thus allowing the states an equitable opportunity of access to human resources for development purpose.

Table 5-4. Demographic Parameters 1985

Country	Crude Birth Rate (per 000)	Crude Death Rate (per 000)	Percent under 15 years	Infant Mortality Rate (per 000)	Natural Increase
Yemen AR	49.6	22.11	47.4	164.0	2.8
PDR Yemen	49.3	8.7	48.2	137.0	3.1
Oman	47.5	15.3	44.1	116.5	3.2
Libya	45.0	11.0	47.0	91.0	3.1
Iraq	43.8	7.9	45.7	81.9	3.6
Syria	43.0	8.3	49.2	60.0	3.5
Saudia Arabia	41.8	12.6	44.7	110.0	2.7
Jordan	41.5	6.7	48.1	63.1	3.5
Morocco	40.0	14.0	46.0	98.0	2.6
Iran	40.0	10.0	45.3	100.0	3.1
Algeria	39.5	8.9	47.1	107.0	3.1
Egypt	37.4	10.9	39.0	104.5.	2.7
Bahrain	36.8	5.9	33.0	44.1	3.1
United Arab Emirates	34.9	3.8	28.4	42.2	3.1
Tunisia	33.0	9.0	40.0	83.0	2.5
Kuwait	32.9	3.7	39.9	23.8	2.9
Turkey	31.0	9.0	39.7	82.0	1.9
Qatar	30.2	6.6	36.2	46.6	2.4
Lebanon	29.8	8.8	49.6	44.4	2.1
Israel	24.0	7.0	33.2	14.0	2.3

Source: Peter Beaumont, G. Blake, and J. Wagstaff, *The Middle East: A Geographical Study*, 2nd ed. (New York: Halsted Press, 1988), p. 189.

Figure 5-9. Estimated Population Distribution by Age and Sex, 1987

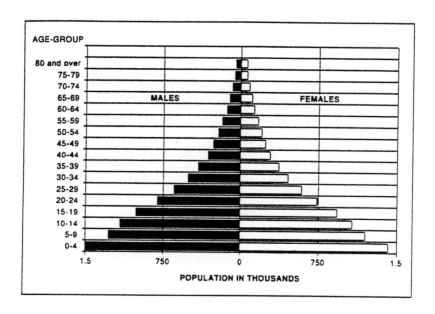

Source: Helen Chapin Metz, *Iraq: A Country Study*, Federal Research Division, Library of Congress, 1990, p. 80.

CHAPTER 6.

Governmental Structure and Representation

The Present Structure and Powers

Presently, Iraq is a unitary system under which all the powers emanate from a single national government. At the peak of the authority stands the Revolutionary Command Council which "is the supreme institution in the state."[1]

The Revolutionary Command Council (RCC), by a two-thirds majority vote of its members, exercises the following powers:

1. Electing a RCC President from its members who is also President of the Republic.
2. Electing a RCC Vice President who is also a national Vice President.
3. Selecting new members for the Council from members of the regional leadership of the Socialist Arab Baath Party.
4. Taking a decision concerning the resignation of the President, Vice President, or any of the Council's members.
5. Accusing and prosecuting members of the Revolutionary Command Council, Vice Presidents and relieving any member form the Council's membership.[2]

Meetings and debates of the Revolutionary Command Council are closed. "Disclosing it, invokes constitutional responsibility before the Council."[3]

Laws and decisions are ratified in the Council by the majority vote of its members, except otherwise prescribed by the Constitution.[4]

The Revolutionary Command Council

1. issues laws and decrees having the force of the law.
2. makes decisions necessary for the execution of the enacted laws.[5]
3. ratifies the defense and public security matters.
4. declares war, total or partial public mobilization, and decides the truce and conclusion of the peace.
5. ratifies the draft general budget of the state and other independent and investment budgets and approves the final accounts.
6. elaborates the rules regarding the prosecution of its members and the judicial procedure to be followed.[6]

The President of the Revolutionary Command Council presides over the meetings of the Council, signs all laws and decisions issued by the Council, publishes them in the official gazette, and issues orders for expenditures.

The National Council and the Legislative Process

The National Council is composed of the people's representatives from various political, economic and social sectors.[8] It is held in two ordinary sessions each year but the President can call it for a special session.[9] All sessions are held and dismissed by a decision of the Revolutionary Command Council.

The National Council considers the bills proposed by the Revolutionary Command Council within 15 days from the date of their delivery to the office of the National Council's President. If the Council approves the bill, it is sent to the President of the Republic to be signed. If the bill is rejected or amended by the National Council, it is returned to the RCC. If the RCC approves the bill as amended, it sends it to the President for its promulgation; if it does not approve the amended bill it returns it to the National Council. In this case the bill will be reviewed in a joint meeting of the two councils which must be passed by two-thirds majority.[10]

If the bill is presented to the National Council by the President of the Republic, the Council considers it within 15 days; if it is rejected, it is returned to the President along with the explanation justifying the rejection.

But, if the Council approves the bill, it is sent to the RCC. If the latter approves it, the bill becomes law. If the National Council amends the bill, it is sent to the RCC which if approved, the bill becomes law.

If the RCC opposes the amended bill, or if it makes its own amendment, the bill is returned to the National Council within a week. If the National Council approves the RCC version, it sends the bill to the President of the Republic to be promulgated.[11]

But if the National Council, during the second reading, sustains its point of view, the bill is considered in the joint meeting of the two councils. If it is approved by a two-thirds majority, it is sent to the President of the Republic for promulgation.

Finally, the National Council also considers bills presented to it by at least one-fourth of its members with exception of the bills related to military, financial, or public security matters.

If the Council approves the bill, it is sent to the RCC to be considered within 15 days. If it approves it, the bill is sent to the President of the Republic for promulgation. If the RCC rejects or amends the bill, it is returned to the National Council.

If the National Council sustains its original point of view then the bill will be considered in a joint meeting of the two councils with two-thirds majority required for its approval.[12]

Two things are of utmost importance to be considered. First, the joint meetings of the two councils are presided over by the President of the Revolutionary Command Council, who is the President of the Republic as well, or by the Vice President who is under the command of the President of the Republic.

Second, the bill must receive a two-thirds majority vote to be approved. Since the RCC has indicated its rejection of the bill it can easily master a one-third plus one to overrule the National Council's supported bill. Therefore the RCC becomes, in essence, the sole law-making body using the National Council essentially as a rubber stamp.

The RCC is not only the main law-making body but it also is the source of major and overall national policies by assuming "the responsibility to realize the public will of the people, by removing the authority from the reactionary, individual and corruptive regime, and returning it to the people."[13]

The Revolutionary Command Council members are not representatives elected by the people but selected by the RCC from the regional leadership of the Socialist Arab Baath Party. Thus the Iraqi Constitution creates a one-party system. Its ruling body is the Revolutionary Command Council over which the party membership has no authority. It chooses its own President who at the same time is the President of the Republic. If one looks at the powers of the President under the Constitution one can easily conclude that the Constitution was written for one-man-rule.

Powers of the Presidency

The President of the Republic is the Head of the State, the Supreme Commander of the Armed forces, and the Chief Executive. He has authority to issue decrees for the exercise of these powers.[15]

What is extraordinary is the following powers given to the President by the Constitution.

1. Preserving the independence of the country, its territorial integrity, safeguarding its internal and external security and protecting the rights and liberties of all citizens.
2. Declaring the state of total and partial emergency and ending it.
3. Appointing the Vice Presidents of the Republic and relieving them of their positions.
4. Appointing the governors, the judges and all civil and military state employees, and terminating their services.
5. Preparing the general plan of the state in all economic and social affairs and referring it to the National Council.
6. Contracting and granting loans, supervising the organization and administration of money and credit.
7. Conducting negotiations and concluding agreements and international treaties.

8. Issuing special amnesty and ratifying judgments of capital punishment.

9. Bringing Vice Presidents and Ministers to trial for functional errors committed by them, for exploiting the authority or for misusing it.[16]

The Interim Constitution was written by the Revolutionary Command Council and cannot be amended except by the same Council. Therefore, the people of Iraq had no input in writing the Constitution and, according to this Interim Constitution, the people of Iraq have no voice in the operation of their government and policy-making process. All the powers are vested in the Revolutionary Command Council and its President who is also the President of the country. Under these two positions, he is the sole authority in the country. There is no trace of democratic representation evident in this constitution.

This concentration of authority in the hands of the Revolutionary Command Council and its power over the socioeconomic and political operation makes the remaining parts of the Constitution ineffective, in effect window dressings. In this regard we refer to the two major areas of this document namely "Fundamental Rights and Duties," and "Social and Economic Foundations of the Iraqi Republic".

In reference to the former, the Constitution states that "Equal opportunities are guaranteed to all citizens according to the law".[17] This is the broadest democratic individual right that a constitution can bestow upon the people. It embodies the grant of equal opportunity in socioeconomic as well as political life to the citizens. In the political arena there is no such right at all. In fact, people have no voice at all. In socioeconomic areas such as health care, education, housing, employment, food, etc., the extent of opportunity depends on the government intention rather than to be based on policies made by the people through a democratic process. This restriction becomes further obvious when the provision ends with "...according to the law." Who makes the law? Not the people or their representatives but the Revolutionary Command Council at the command of the President of the Republic.

The same applies to the other civil rights provisions such as: "An accused is presumed to be innocent, until proved guilty at a legal trial".[18] In actual operation of the system, an accused is guilty unless proved innocent. Tortures or intimidations for confession by the investigating offices are not unusual. "The right of defense is sacred, in all stages of proceeding and presentation."[19] "The dignity of man is safeguarded. It is inadmissible to cause any physical or psychological harm."[20] None of these guarantees were honored by the regime and these individual rights were continually violated as soon as any action was suspected to be anti-regime. "It is inadmissible to arrest a person, to stop him, to imprison him or to search him, except in accordance with the rules of the law..."[21] "Homes have their sanctity. It is inadmissible to enter or search them, except in accordance with the rules of the law." The rights granted under these provisions have no guarantee as long as they are subject to "the rules of the law." where all the laws are made by the Revolutionary Command Council. Necessarily such laws will be beneficial to sustaining of its power and privileges. "The Constitution guarantees freedom of opinion, publication, meeting, demonstrations and formation of political parties, syndicates and societies in accordance with the objectives of the Constitution and within the limits of the law."[23] Again the authority of a constitutional provision is made conditional to the limits of the ordinary law which is not even passed by a representative body but by a self-appointed and self-perpetuated body, namely, Revolutionary Command Council.

"The state ensures the considerateness necessary to exercise these liberties, which comply with the revolutionary, national and progressive trend."[24] This provision simply implies that no liberty will be allowed if it is in conflict with the national programs of action established by the Revolutionary Command Council.

These are just a few examples to demonstrate the uselessness of the Constitution as far as the individual rights are concerned. The Constitution establishes a purely autocratic government, combining the legislative and executive powers and bestowing them in a nonrepresentative body which operates under the command of one man who is at the same time the head of the Council as well as the President of the Republic.

What is missing here is a representative form of government in which all the major groups in Iraq have meaningful participation and responsible contribution. With no doubt the most suitable form of government for Iraq is a federal system and the most appropriate and practical form of federalism, territorially speaking, is the one proposed in Chapter Five consisting of six states and a national territory (Figure 6-1). The most suitable system of government for Iraq is a socialistic representative democracy within the boundaries of Islamic principles. Within these frameworks we now attempt to present and discuss the form and structure of the national and state governments, and the manner of representation, and the extension of their powers.

The New National Government: A Socialistic Representative Democracy

The powers of government in the United Republics of Iraq are the legislative, judicial and executive powers to be exercised in accordance with the Constitution. These powers are functionally independent of each other.[25]

The form of government selected for the United Republics is neither presidential nor parliamentary but a combination from both in order to create a strong executive branch which is a necessity in less developed countries for a dynamic execution of development plans, and yet responsible and answerable to the people through the legislative branch.

The National Legislative Branch

The legislative powers as granted by the Constitution shall be vested in the Legislative Branch of the United Republics of Iraq consisting of a Senate and a House of Representatives. The House of Representatives shall have 165 members on the basis of one representative for each 100,000 population with fractions over 50,000 in any state receiving one representative. Table 6-1 illustrates the share of each state and the share of each district within each state.

The House members shall be elected on the basis of proportional representation by a manner to avoid extreme fragmentation of the electorate into miniature political parties. Such a fragmentation will cause serious democratic coalition problems in forming a majority government similar to the problems facing Israel and Italy. To achieve this goal and eliminate the extreme political fragmentation, the appropriate way appears to be to allow proportional representation but divide each district within the state into electoral districts allowing

Figure 6-1. Iraq: States and Federal Territory

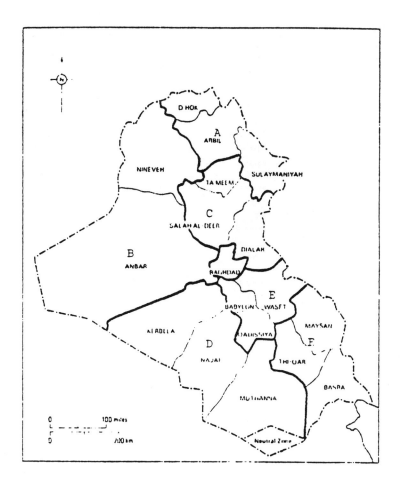

Table 6-1. Distribution of Seats of the House of the Representatives and Electoral Districts Among the States and Baghdad

State	No. of Seats	Districts	No. of Seats	No. of Electoral Districts	Seats
A	20	Dahuk	3	1	3
		Arbil	7	2	3 & 4
		Sulaymaniyah	9	3	3 each
		At large	1	-	-
B	23	Ninevah	15	5	3 each
		Anber	8	2	4 each
C	22	Tamin	6	2	3 each
		Salah ad Din	7	2	3 & 4
		Diyala	9	3	3 each
D	15	Karbala	5	1	5
		Najaf	7	2	3 & 4
		Muthanna	3	1	3
E	22	Qadissiya	6	2	3 each
		Wasit	5	1	5
		Babylon	11	3	3, 4 & 4
F	23	Maysan	5	1	5
		Dhi Qar	9	3	3 each
		Basra	9	3	3 each
Baghdad	17	Ward 1	3	1	3
		Ward 2	3	1	3
		Ward 3	3	1	3
		Wasd 4	4	1	4
		Ward 5	4	1	4
	21	Ward 1	4	1	4
		Ward 2	4	1	4
		Ward 3	4	1	4
		Ward 4	4	1	4
		Ward 5	5	1	5
	Total		163		

three representatives be chosen at large from each. Exceptionally, up to five representatives may be allowed to some electoral districts but never less than three. For example, Arbil may be divided into two electoral districts of three and four representatives with a total of seven; Anber into two electoral districts each having four representatives; Karbala, Muthanna, Wasit, and Maysan each forming only one electoral district with five representatives each. Table 6-1 illustrates the number of seats in the House of Representatives for each state and district as well as the number of electoral districts allocated to each district within each state.

Despite the fact that Baghdad is a national territory its residents shall have representation in both houses of legislation. It would be unfair to exclude nearly four million citizens of the country, about one-fifth of the population, from representation and participation in the policy-making process.

Special seats also may be allowed for ethnic and religious minorities scattered around the country. Otherwise these citizens will be without representation and will have no voice in the government. For example, the Constitution of the Islamic Republic of Iran (Art. 64) prescribes that "The Zoroastrians and Jews shall have one representative each; The Assyrian and Chaldean Christians shall together have one representative; and the Armenian Christians of the South and North shall each elect one representative to the Islamic Assembly." In the case of Iraq this minority representation should be based on one representation for each 100,000 from each minority group or its fraction over 50,000.

There are a variety of formulas for proportional representation. The method used in Israel seems quite appropriate, except that the extremely minor parties which have complicated the majority rule through proper coalition in Israel will not exist under the above proposed electoral method.

To be elected for the House of Representative one must be 25 years of age, a citizen of the United Republics of Iraq for at least ten years, and a resident of the district from which to be elected. The term of the office shall be four years with one-half of the membership to be elected every two years as follows:

The representatives from the states of A,B, and C, shall be initially elected for four years. This comprises a total of 65 seats. The representatives from the states of D, E, and F, shall be initially elected for two years. After serving two years the next elections for this group shall be for a four year term. This comprises a total of 60 seats. Seventeen of the 28 representatives from Baghdad shall be elected for four years and the remaining 21 for two years. After serving these two years and thereafter, they shall be elected for four years.

No representative can by reelected to the House of Representatives for more than three full terms or a total of 12 years. These terms do not have to be consecutive. However, a person, after serving for 12 years may again run for the office after a lapse of eight years.

When a vacancy happens in the House of Representatives from any state, the Governor of that state shall issue an order of appointment of a person of his selection to fill such vacancy for the remaining of the affected term.

The House of Representatives shall choose its speaker and other officers, and shall establish its own internal operations and procedures in accordance with the provisions of the Constitution.

The President and the ministers have the authority to attend the sessions of the House of Representatives collectively or individually. They may also have their aids and advisors accompany them. If deemed necessary by the members, the President and the ministers shall attend the House, and shall be granted audience upon their request.[26]

The President before addressing himself to any other business must obtain a vote of confidence on behalf of the Council of Ministers, after its creation and introduction to the House of Representatives. The vote of confidence is established when supported by the simple majority vote of the representatives. During his incumbency, the President shall also seek a vote of confidence on behalf of the ministers whenever facing difficult and controversial issues.[27]

Whenever at least one-third of the representatives of the House of Representatives asks a question relating to the duties of the President, or whenever at least one-fourth of the representatives of the same House ask a question relating to the duties of a Cabinet Minister, the President or the Minister shall be present at the House and answer the question. The reply should be given in a period not exceeding one month in the case of the President and ten days in the case of the Minister, unless there is a valid reason for delay which is accepted by the House of Representatives.[28]

The House of Representatives shall have the sole Power of Impeachment of any national officer of the Executive or Judicial branches including the President of the United Republics. A motion for impeachment of a national officer can proceed if requested by at least one-fourth of the representatives of the House in writing.[29]

The Cabinet or the Minister involved shall report to the House within ten days after the call for impeachment and shall request a vote of confidence from the House. If the ministers or the Minister in question are not present to answer the charges, then representatives who have moved for impeachment shall provide the necessary explanations and, if deemed necessary by the House, a vote of no confidence will be cast.

If the House arrives at a vote of no confidence by a two-thirds majority vote, then the Council of Ministers or the Minister will be dismissed. Members of the impeached Cabinet or the individual Minister cannot participate in the subsequent Council of Ministers that is to be formed.

In the event that at least one-third of the members of the House of Representatives should move for the impeachment of the President in relation to the performance of his executive duties, then the President shall report to the House within one month from the date of the motion for impeachment, and shall provide adequate explanations for his actions. If, after hearing the arguments for and against the impeachment, two-thirds of the members of the House should issue a vote of no confidence, the decision will be presented to the Senate. If, after hearing the President in defense of his position, two-thirds of the members of the Senate should issue a vote of no confidence,[30] then the President will be obliged to resign. In this case the Vice President, if there is no Vice President, then the Speaker of the House of Representatives shall take the office of Presidency as President until the next presidential election.

Judgement in cases of impeachment shall not extend further than to removal from office and disqualification to hold and enjoy any important national office and benefits from the previous office held. However, the party dismissed through impeachment shall be liable and subject to judicial proceedings, judgment, and punishment if any of his actions has been in violation of law.

The House of the Senate

Representation in the Senate shall be on the basis of equality of the states regardless of population size or economic resources. Even though the states have nearly equal voice in the House of Representatives and from that viewpoint their influence in the Senate will be more or less the same, the National District of Baghdad will substantially loose the significant power it will enjoy in the House of representatives. This difference alone is a very important reason for the formation of the Senate in which the National District of Baghdad will have the same voice as any one of the six states. This will establish a power relationship on equal basis between the states and the national government at the national level.

The Senate shall be composed of 28 senators. Each state as well as the National District of Baghdad shall have four senators elected at large from each State and Baghdad through the method of proportional representation.

The term of the Senate shall be four years, one-half, 14, to be elected every two years as follows: The initial election of the senators from the States A, B, and C, shall be for four years, and those from the States D, E, and F, for two years. Two senators from Baghdad shall be elected for four years and the other two for two years. From there on each senator will be up for reelection after serving his/her four year term.

To be elected as a Senator, one must be 30 years of age, a citizen of the United Republics of Iraq for ten years, and a resident of the state from which to be elected. No Senator can be reelected to the Senate for more than three full terms or a total of 12 years. These terms do not have to be consecutive.

The Senate shall choose its President and other officers, and shall established its own internal operations and procedures in accordance with the provisions of the Constitution.

When a vacancy happens in the Senate representation from any State, the Governor of that state shall issue an order of appointment of a person of his selection to fill such vacancy for the rest of the affected term.

The Senate shall have the sole power to try the impeachment of the President of the United Republics sustained by the House of

Representatives. When convened for this purpose, the Senators shall be on Oath of Affirmation. The Chief Justice of the Supreme Court of the United Republics shall preside the proceedings. No President shall be dismissed from the office without the affirmative vote of two-thirds of the Senators present.

General Provisions and Powers
of the Legislative Branch

The time place and manner of holding elections for Senators and Representatives, shall be prescribed in each state by its legislature, but the National Legislature may at any time by law make or alter such regulations.[31]

Each House shall be the judge of elections, returns, and qualifications of its own members. A majority of each House shall constitute a quorum to do business, but a smaller number may adjourn from day to day. Each House shall establish rules for attendance, manners, and penalties by which to compel the attendance of the absent members.[32]

Each House may determine the rules of its proceedings, punish its members for disorderly or unethical conduct, and with the concurrence of two-thirds majority, expel a member after a proper hearing.

Each House shall keep a journal of its proceedings which will be published or made public through other media. The Yes and No votes of the members of either House on any question shall, at the desire of one-tenth of those present, be entered on the journal.[33]

Neither House, during the session of the Legislature, shall, without the consent of the other, adjourn for more than three days, nor to any other place than that in which the two Houses shall be sitting.[34]

The members of the National Legislature shall receive a compensation for their services, to be ascertained by law, and paid out of the Treasury of the United Republics of Iraq. As elected legislators they shall not be eligible to any retirement benefits; this is the right of only the permanent members of the government such as civil servants. Except in the cases of treason, felony, and breach of the peace, they shall be privileged from arrest during their attendance at the session of their respective Houses, in going and returning from the same; and for any speech or debate in either House, they shall not be questioned in any other place.[35]

No Senator or Representative shall, during the time for which he was elected, be appointed to any civil office under the authority of the United Republics of Iraq, which shall have been created, or the emoluments whereof shall have been increased during such time, and no person holding any office under the United Republics shall be a member of either House during his continuance in office.[36]

All bills shall be approved by both the House of Representatives and the Senate and shall be presented to the President of the United Republics. If he approves, he shall sign it and the bill becomes a law. If he approves certain parts and does not approve others, the parts approved become a law and the parts vetoed he shall return with his objections to the House of Representatives for reconsideration. If after such reconsideration two-thirds of the House agrees to pass any vetoed part, it shall be sent along with the objection of the President of the United Republics to the Senate for the same reconsideration. Any vetoed part approved by the House of Representatives and two-thirds majority of the Senators present, shall become a law. In all such cases the names of the members voting for or against the bill shall be entered on the Journal of each House respectively. If any bill is not returned by the President of the United Republics within ten working days (weekend, holyday excepted) after it is presented to him, it shall become a law the same as he had signed it.[37]

Every order, resolution, or vote to which the concurrence of the Senate and House of Representatives is necessary (except on the question of adjournment) shall be presented to the President of the United Republics and shall be subject to the same procedures prescribed above for a bill.

The Legislative Branch shall have the following powers:

1. To establish and collect taxes, duties, imposts and excises, to pay the debts and provide for the common defense and general welfare of the United Republics. However, all taxes, duties, imposts, and excises must be uniform throughout the Republics.
2. To borrow money on the credit of the United Republics.
3. To regulate commerce with foreign nations, and among the Republics.

4. To establish uniform rules of naturalization, and uniform laws on the subject of bankruptcies throughout the Republics.
5. To produce money, regulate the value thereof and of foreign exchange, and fix the standards of weights and measures.
6. To provide for the punishment of counterfeiting the securities and the currency.
7. To promote the progress of science, literature, and arts, by securing for limited times to authors and inventors the exclusive right to their respective writing and discoveries.
8. To declare war and make rules concerning captures on national land and water. This means that the President of the United Republics cannot go into war without approval of the Legislative Branch except when the country is attacked from the outside; in which case the military action will be restricted to the defense of the nation and in due course, without delay, the President must report and receive the consent of the Legislative Branch.
9. To raise and support armed forces. This means that the Legislative Branch and not the President determines the size and combination of the armed forces but the President has the command of the forces. At the same time the Legislative Branch makes rules for the governing and regulating of the armed forces.
10. To provide for calling fourth the State militia (state national guard) to execute the laws of the United Republics, suppress insurrections and repel invasion. The Legislative Branch may delegate this power to the President of the United Republics.
11. To provide for organizing, arming and disciplining, the militia, and for governing such parts of them as may be employed in the service of the United Republics, reserving to the States respectively, the appointment of the officers, and the authority of training the militia according to the discipline prescribed by the Legislative Branch. This allows each State to have full authority over its own military forces, composed of army and air force, except when the national government takes over the command to supplement the national armed forces for national services such as defense or suppression of insurrection.
12. To exercise exclusive legislation in all cases whatsoever, over the Special District of Baghdad which shall remain under the

domain of the National Government, as the Seat of the United Republics. To exercise like authority over all places, purchased by the consent of the Legislature of the State in which the same property is located, necessary for the expansion of the national services to the State population and for the appropriate operation of certain national function such as establishment of military bases for recruitment, training, and production of military materials.

13. To make all laws necessary and proper for carrying into execution the foregoing powers and all other powers vested by the Constitution in the government of the United Republics, or in any department or office thereof.[38]

The privilege of the Writ of Habeas Corpus shall not be suspended, unless when public safety may require it in cases of rebellion or invasion.[39]

No money shall be drawn from the Treasury, without appropriation made by law, and a regular statement and account of the receipts and expenditures of all public money shall be published from time to time.[40]

Membership in the Legislature is vested in the individual, and is not transferable. The Legislature cannot delegate the authority to enact legislation to an individual or committee.[41] Moreover, the Legislature can, in accordance with provisions of the Constitution, delegate the responsibility for permanent ratification of the charter of organizations, corporations, public or semi-public agencies, to relevant committees or proper governmental authorities. These acts cannot be in contrast to the common laws of the country.[42]

CHAPTER 7.

The Executive and Judicial Branches, State and Local Government

The National Executive Branch

The Executive Power shall be vested in a President of the United Republics of Iraq. He shall hold his office during the term of six years, and together with the Vice President, chosen for the same term, be elected by popular vote the process of which shall be established by the National Legislature.

To be elected for the office of President or Vice President, the candidate must receive at least 50 percent of the votes cast; if no candidate receives this required 50 percent of votes, there shall be a rerun of elections between the two candidates with the highest percentage of votes, and the one receiving 50 percent or more shall be elected.

No person except a natural born citizen shall be eligible to the office of President or Vice President, neither shall any person be eligible to that office who shall not have attained the age of 35 years and has been 15 years accumulatively a resident within the United Republics.[1]

In case of removal of the President from office, or his death, resignation, or inability to discharge the powers and duties of the said office, the same shall devolve on the Vice President, and the Legislature may by law provide for the case of removal, death, resignation or inability, both of the President and Vice President, declaring what officer shall then act as President, and such officer shall act accordingly, until the disability be removed or a new President shall be elected.[2] In the United States, the Congress has determined the succession order to the office of President in the following order: Vice President, Speaker of the House of Representatives, President Pro-Tem of the Senate, Secretary of State, and Secretary of Defense.

The President shall, at stated times, receive for his services, a compensation, which can neither be increased nor diminished during the period for which he shall have been elected, and he shall not receive within that period any other emolument from the United Republics, or any of them.[3]

Before he enters on the execution of his office, he shall take the following oath in a joint session of the Legislatures administered by the Chief Justice of the Supreme Court of the United Republics:

In the name of God, the Compassionate, the Merciful, I as President, pledge before the Holy Quran and the people of the United Republics of Iraq, and to the Almighty and Exalted God, that I shall protect Islam as the official religion, the order of the United Republics, and the Constitution of the country; that I shall exploit all of my talents and abilities for the fulfillment of the responsibilities that I have assumed; that I will dedicate myself to the service of the people and the betterment of the country; that I will promote morality and faith and support truth and justice; that I will abstain from all forms of self-indulgence; that I will protect the freedom, dignity and constitutional rights of all citizens; that I will not spare any efforts to protect the national frontiers and the political, economic, and cultural independence of the country; that in seeking assistance from God and following in the path of the Prophet of Islam, I, as a pious and selfless trustee, will preserve the power vested in me by the people as a sacred trust; and that I will entrust that power to a person elected after me by the people."[4]

Unlike the Constitution of the United States where the grant of presidential powers is very general, in Iraq like in any other less developed country, this grant of powers by the Constitution must be clear and specific. This is because, as historically proven, in less developed countries the President has a tendency to assume more and more power which often undermines democratic norms and principles and leads toward authoritarianism. The President has much less opportunity to abuse his constitutional powers when his powers are specifically designated in the Constitution. To avoid deterioration of a constitutional democracy, among others, the Constitution must contain provision similar to the following.

The President, with respect to duties and responsibilities bestowed on him by the Constitution or other laws, shall be responsible to the people and the Legislature.[5]

The President, for the performance of his executive duties, may have assistants. The first assistant to the President shall have the responsibility of administering the affairs of the Cabinet of Ministers, and coordinating the functions of the other assistants, subject to approval by the President.[6]

The President shall be responsible for national planning, national budget, and the administrative and personnel matters. He may entrust the management of such matters to another authority within his administration.[7]

In special circumstances, and subject to the approval of the Cabinet of Ministers, the President may appoint one or more special representatives with specific authorities. In such cases, the decisions of the representative or representatives shall have the same effect as those of the President and the Cabinet.[8]

The President confirms the appointment of the ambassadors recommended by the foreign Minister. The President shall sign the credentials of the Iraqi ambassadors and shall receive the credentials of foreign ambassadors.[9]

The President shall head the Council of Ministers and shall supervise the work of the Ministers. He shall coordinate the activities of the Ministers and with their assistance shall determine the governmental programs and policies, and shall enforce the law.

In the event of conflict of opinion, or in matters of interference in the constitutional duties of governmental agencies, the decision of the Council of Ministers based on the recommendation of the President, shall be binding, except when a modification or a new interpretation of the laws is warranted. The President is responsible to the House of Representatives for the actions of the Council of Ministers.[10]

The Cabinet Ministers shall remain in office unless they are dismissed by the President, or are denied a vote of confidence by the House of Representatives.

Resignation of the Cabinet or an individual Minister shall be submitted to the President. The Cabinet Ministers shall continue to perform their duties until such time as a new Cabinet or Minister is designated and approved by the House of Representatives.

The President can appoint a caretaker administrator, for a period of three month , to any government ministry which has a vacant ministerial position.[11]

The President can dismiss the Cabinet Ministers. In such a case a vote of confidence for the new Minister or Ministers must be obtained from the House of Representatives. If half of the members of the Cabinet are changed after a vote of confidence has been obtained, the President must seek a new vote of confidence for his entire Cabinet.[12]

Each Minister is responsible to the President and the House of Representatives for the functions of his ministry; but he shall also be responsible for the actions of other Ministers in matters that have been approved by the entire Cabinet.[13]

In addition to cases where the cabinet or an individual minister is empowered to draft executive regulations for the enforcement of a law, the Cabinet is also entitled to issue other decrees or regulations in order to fulfill administrative duties, safeguard the execution of the laws and regulate administrative organizations. Each of the Ministers is also entitled, with the approval of the Cabinet and within the framework of his duties, to formulate regulations and issue directives. The content of these regulations should not conflict with the wording or the spirit of the law.

The Cabinet can delegate some of its responsibilities to commissions consisting of several Ministers. The decision of such commissions, within the framework of the law, and upon the endorsement of the President, shall be binding.[14]

Investigation of charges against the President, the presidential deputies, or the Ministers, with regard to common crimes shall be conducted by the Ministry of Justice and tried in the public courts with the prior knowledge of the House of Representatives.[15]

The President, his deputies, Ministers, and government employees may not hold more than one position within government. They are also forbidden to hold employment in organizations whose capital is wholly or partially provided by the government, nor can they hold the position of Representative of the House or the Senate, or seek the position of an attorney or legal counsel. They also cannot assume the presidency or the directorship of any private corporation, except for governmental corporations. Positions in teaching at universities or research institutions are exempted from the provisions of this article.[16]

Provisions in relation to double or multiple employment is important to be made part of the constitution because in nearly all less developed countries many governmental officials, especially those in the upper ranks, have more than one position in the government some of which they attend only on the pay day to receive their salary. Furthermore, many employees also have jobs in the private sector for which they have to be totally responsible otherwise they lose the job. Consequently, they pay the least possible attention to their governmental duties. This is a major cause of inefficiency and lack of productive and responsible services. Teaching at universities is an honor even for a Minister. They are welcome at universities because of their vast knowledge and experience in foreign and governmental affairs.

The assets of the President, his aids, Cabinet Ministers, their wives and children, shall be investigated by the Department of Justice, before and after their tenure in office, so that they may not have been augmented unlawfully.[17]

This is a unique provision in the Constitution of the Islamic Republic of Iran, and a very appropriate one. It is not unusual for the President, Ministers, and other upper level governmental officials to enrich themselves from the public treasury and government contracts.

The President shall be Commander in Chief of the armed forces, and the militia of the several states when called into the actual service of the United Republics. He may require the opinion, in writing, of the principal officer in each of the executive ministries, upon any subject relating to the duties of their respective offices. He shall have power to grant reprieves and pardons for offenses against the United Republics, except in cases of impeachment.[18]

The president shall have power to make treaties with the approval of the majority of the Senators. He shall nominate, and by and with the advice and consent of the Senate, shall appoint justices of the Supreme Court, and all judges to other national courts.[19] He shall take care that the laws be faithfully executed.

The President shall, at least once a year, give to the joint session of the Legislature information of the State of the Union, Economy, and Budget, and recommend to their consideration such measures as he shall judge necessary and expedient.[20]

He may, on extraordinary occasions, convene both Houses, or either of them; and with respect to the time of adjournment, he may adjourn them to such time as he shall think proper.

The Judicial Branch

The judicial power of the United Republics shall be independent in its operation from the Executive and Legislative branches. Thus, it shall not be under the administrative command of the Ministry of Justice such as the case is at the present.

The judicial power of the United Republics shall be vested in one Supreme Court, and such intermediary and lower courts as the Legislature from time to time may ordain and establish.

The judges, both of the Supreme and inferior courts, shall hold their offices for a term of 12 years in good behavior and may be reappointed for another term. They shall, at stated times, receive for their services, a compensation, which shall not be diminished during their continuance in office.[21]

The judicial power shall extend to all cases, in law and equity, arising under the Constitution, the laws of the United Republics, and treaties properly concluded as prescribed in the Constitution; to all cases affecting Ambassadors, other public Ministers and Consuls; to all cases of admiralty and maritime Jurisdiction; to controversies to which the United Republics shall be a party; to controversies between two or more States; between citizens of the same state in claims affected by the laws of different states.[22]

In all cases affecting Ambassadors, other public Ministers and Consuls, and those in which a State shall be party, the Supreme Court shall have original jurisdiction. In all the other cases before maintained, the Supreme Court shall have appellate jurisdiction, both as to law and fact, with such acceptance, and under such regulations as the Legislature shall make.[23]

The trial of all crimes shall be held in the state where the same crimes shall have been committed; but when not committed within any State, the trial shall be at such place or places as the Legislature may by law have directed.

Since as in many other Third World Countries the Middle Eastern countries apply the Civil Law or Continental Law system, in contrast to Anglo-American law, trial by jury is not a familiar aspect of the judicial system. In some countries the jury system is allowed only in political trials. The grand jury system used in the United States is not recognized in nearly all Third World countries; in fact it is a quite unfamiliar function.

The Supreme Court is established in order to ensure the proper enforcement of the Constitution and the laws by the courts, to guarantee the uniformity of the judicial procedures and application of the Constitution through judicial review power over the decisions of the national courts in all matters as well as the highest State courts on constitutional issues.

In less developed countries the experience shows that often the legislative body becomes a rubber stamp for the Chief Executive. Iraq will not be an exception when it moves from its present authoritarian regime to representative democracy. Precautions inducive to avoid a national executive influence have been taken here first by establishing a federal system where each state shall have its own autonomous government, shall pass and execute its own laws within the framework established by the Constitution. Most of the citizens' needs for government will be satisfied through the State government. This will substantially reduce the need for national authority. Furthermore, the Constitution makes the President and his Cabinet subject to substantial check by the Legislature through the authority to question the activities of the Executive Branch and subject it to a vote of nonconfidence in the case of improper activities and abuse of power. Finally, the system needs an institution as the guardian of the Constitution and its sole interpreter such as a Supreme Court. By this constitutional authority the Court will be able to check the Legislative Branch as well as the states so that the Constitution will be respected, properly executed and will not be abused. This will have utmost importance in regard to individual rights which are usually easily abused in nearly all less developed countries. Iraq, in particular, has suffered a great deal in this regard.

The Chief Justice of the Supreme Court and the Attorney General must be just and learned persons, and must possess knowledge of the judicial matters. The Attorney General shall be appointed for a term of six years by the President with the approval of the Senate.[24]

The judicial independence requires that the judges may not be temporarily or permanently suspended without a trial, impeachment, or evidence of guilt, or an offense that warrants dismissal. Nor can the judges be transferred or given new assignments, unless warranted by the best interests of the society and in accordance with the decision of the Chief Justice of the Supreme Court who is also the Chief Administrator of the Judicial Branch. The rotation of the tour of the duty of the judges will be in accordance to law.[25]

For the purposes of investigating the petitions, grievances, and complaints by the citizens against government officials, agencies, and regulations, there shall be established a Tribunal of Administrative Justice subject to judicial review by the Supreme Court. The authority and mode of operation of the Tribunal shall be defined by law.[26]

This kind of tribunal is quite familiar in the countries under the Civil Law system including several countries in Europe. The purpose is to accelerate the proceeding and to subject the complaints against the government to a specialized Tribunal.

There shall be an Office of Judicial Administration which operates under the supervision of the Chief Justice of the Supreme Court. It shall have a Director and other officials appointed as prescribed by law and independent from the Executive Branch. It shall have authority over the administration of non-judicial personnel of the Judicial Branch.

Based on the authority of the Ministry of Justice to ensure the proper conduct of affairs and to enforce the correct implementation of the law in government agencies, an organization by the name of Office of General Inspectorate, under supervision of the Minister of Justice shall be established. The Office shall also respond to investigative directions from the House of Representatives relating to proper implementation of the laws and shall report directly to the House. The jurisdiction and duties of this organization shall be defined by law.

This aspect of the functions of the Office shall be similar to the General Accounting Office in the United States which is an independent organization created by Congress to supervise governmental operation, have a periodic investigation of selected agencies and report its findings to Congress as well as to the public.

The Legislature may establish, if it deems appropriate, special courts to deal with certian aspects of the Islamic and other minority religious laws or delegate such funcitons to the ordinary courts.

All judicial officers must be academically well acquainted with the Islamic principles and laws.

General Provisions

The Constitution should start with a Preamble stating in general terms the purposes and aims of the government, a statement similar to the following:

> We the People of the United Republics of Iraq, in order to form a perfect Union, establish social and legal justice, insure domestic tranquility, provide for common defense, promote the general welfare, and secure the blessings of liberty to ourselves and our posterity, do ordain and establish this Constitution of the United Republics of Iraq.[27]

The flag of the United Republics of Iraq, its Emblem, and stipulations concerning the two, are regulated by law.[28]

The United Republics of Iraq is a Sovereign People's democratic Union composed of Six Independent Republics, as prescribed by this Constitution, and a National Government. [29]

The people are the source of authority and its legitimacy.[30] Islam is the religion of the country.[31] Some scholars may think that there is no need to state the religion of Islam in this Constitution since it is a matter of fact that over some 90 percent of the population are Muslims. But the provisions of this Constitution have been formulated with neighboring Iran in mind, which adheres to Islamic fundamentalism, and with intention to minimize, if not alleviate, future criticism in regard to the nature of this Constitution and the country's political system. For this purpose also, whenever proper, many provisions of this Constitution have been adopted, with some modifications, from the 1988 Constitution of the Islamic Republic of Iran.

This Constitution acknowledges the legitimate rights of all minorities within the territories of the States and the Nation including the right for proportional representation.[32]

Arabic is the official language of the United Republics. The Kurdish and other minority languages are also recognized.[33]

The City of Baghdad is the Capital of the United Republics of Iraq. The District of Baghdad is the territory under the authority of the National Government.

State Governments

The Constitution guarantees to every State a social-democratic representative form of government with the structure and functions that are within the framework of, but not necessarily similar to, those of the national government.

The State Constitution

Each state shall establish its own constitution as desired by the people of the state and shall determine the manner of its amendment and ratification. No provision of the state constitution may be in contrast or conflict with the provisions of the national constitution.

The individual rights and freedoms embodied in the state constitution may extend such rights and freedoms beyond those guaranteed by the national constitution.

The residents of the United Republics of Iraq are free to move from one state or national territory of Baghdad into another state and assume residence therein. Once moved into another state they become subject to all laws of that state, such as payment of taxes for their earnings within the state. The resident of any state may seek employment in another. The formal requirements for residency shall be established by state law on the basis of uniformity without discrimination against any person on account of race, religion, sex, national origin, or group affiliation. Such freedom of movement is essential for national solidarity and effective economic development.

The following are the limitations on state powers:

No state shall enter into any treaty, alliance, or confederation; coin money; pass any bill of attainer or ex post facto law.[34]

No state shall, without consent of the national legislature, lay any imposts or duties on imports or exports, except what may be absolutely necessary for executing its inspection laws; and the net produce of all duties and imposts, laid by any state on imports and exports, shall be for the use of the Treasury of the United Republics, and all such laws shall be subject to the revision and control of the national legislature.[35]

No state shall, without consent of the national legislature, keep military troops in time of peace, enter into any agreement or compact with another state, or with a foreign country, or engage in war, unless actually invaded, or in such imminent danger as will not admit of delay.[36]

Each state may levy taxes on its residents and raise revenues to pay for the operation of its government and administration and execution of its general welfare programs such as education and health care and other programs.

The national government serves as a model for the state governments. Accordingly, the constitutions and political structures of the states tend to resemble that of the national government. Like the national constitution, state constitutions include bill of rights that set forth the rights of the individuals that are to be preserved against infringement by the state. They also provide for the formal separation of powers and distribution of authority among the legislative, executive and judicial branches of the state government.

The state government is closer to the people than the national government, and most of the individual's daily life is affected and regulated by the state constitution, laws, regulations, and judicial decisions. Accordingly, the state constitutions are formulated in more detailed manner for the purpose of restraining state authority on infringement upon individual rights. Thus, state powers are more narrowly and explicitly defined in contrast to a broad definition of the individual rights. These constitutions may contain specific stipulations about the operation of government, rather than defining powers and limitations in a general way. As in the United States, state constitutions may include specific provisions on taxation and finance tending to impose limitation on the government's authority to tax or borrow money. As a consequence, in the United States, the length of constitutions vary from about 7,000 words of the National Constitution to approximately 174,000 words of the state of Alabama Constitution.

For this reason, many specific provisions of the state constitutions may become outdated by the passage of time and changes in socioeconomic conditions and must be altered by constitutional amendments. For example, in the United States, the constitution of Hawaii has had 78 amendments since 1950; that of New York, 205 since 1895; and that of Texas, 304 since 1876. In contrast, the National Constitution, which was written in general terms, has had only 26 amendments in more than 200 years. From these the first ten amendments, known as the Bill of Rights, were a part of the original constitution and intentionally left out to facilitate the ratification of the original constitution and were added to it immediately thereafter in the form of amendments. Two amendments (11th and 16th) were passed to overrule the U.S. Supreme Court's decisions; another two (18th and 21st) related to prohibition on producing, transferring, and sale of alcoholic beverages, the latter abolishing the former. Thus, discarding all these 14 amendments, it is appropriate to say that since its ratification in the late 18th century, the U.S. Constitution has had only 12 actual amendments. This unique characteristic makes the U.S. Constitution an exception, compared to all existing constitutions in the world today.

There are two ways to amend a state constitution. The first method is through the state legislature. In this case the amendment is introduced by one or a group of legislators. After receiving a two-thirds majority vote in the House of Representatives, the amendment is proposed for ratification to the voters of the state. It requires a majority vote of the electorate to ratify an amendment.

The second method is through the state constitutional convention. There are two ways to call for the formation of a constitutional convention. The state legislature may propose it. In this case the issue is submitted to the popular vote. A majority support is required. Another way is through the initiative petition. When a certain percentage of the voters, e.g. five percent, as prescribed by the state constitution, sign and present a petition to the state legislature to call for a constitutional convention, the subject is submitted to popular vote. The convention is formed as soon as its formation is approved by the majority of the electorate. These methods of amendments and all related provisions are included in the state constitution.

The Legislative Branch

Each state has a House of Representatives the structure, function, and manner of representation are established by the state constitution. The representation is based on population in each electoral district based on equality of voters. The system of elections is proportional representation from multiple seat districts in order to guarantee proper minority group representation in the state legislature. The manner and method of such representation are established by the state constitution or laws.

Each state exercises power over its residents which includes passing laws and execution of laws, maintaining law and order, enacting taxes and raising revenues. This authority of the states extend to every aspect of life within the state except those granted to the national government.

Although constitutional provisions of the states are similar to one another in broad outline, substantial variations may exist in specific details. State legislatures differ in size. Based on the present population of states, the appropriate representation seems to be one representation for every 20,000 population. This will place the average size of the state house of representatives at about 100. The size of the legislature in the states having more than two million population will exceed this number and in those with less than two million will be less than 100.

However, each state may determine the size of its legislature in its constitution or base it on population per seat. The latter method will automatically change the size of the legislature by increase or decrease in the state population.

In any case, the representation must be based on equality of votes. This means that the state must be either divided into electoral districts with nearly equal population, or, if the population varies from district to district, the size of representation per seat must be equal in all districts, for example, 20,000 population per seat. Thus, a district having 60,000 population and another 80,000 must have three and four representatives respectively. The method of proportional representation requires multiple seat districts in a manner that it would not cause extreme fragmentation of the electorate into miniature political factions. No district should be established which allows less than three seats at large. The method of proportional representation proposed for national elections is proper to be used as a model.

The powers of the state legislature include but is not restricted to:

1. To make all laws necessary and proper for carrying out all the powers vested by the state constitution in the state government.
2. To establish and collect taxes, fees and duties, to pay debts and provide for law and order and general welfare of the state population.
3. To borrow money on the credit of the state.
4. To regulate commerce within the state.
5. To provide for organization, training, and maintaining of the State Militia within the framework of standards and limitations established by the national legislature.
6. To establish its own governmental organization and operation.
7. To determine the size and general functions of the executive organizations leaving the governor the authority to organize and reorganize them.

Members of the legislature are elected for a four year term with a 12 year limit with the procedures similar to those of the national legislature.

The state legislature determines the salary of its members and staff. It should not be excessive and must be comparable to salaries of other state's top officials. It also approves the salary schedule proposed by the executive branch for the government officials and employees.

Bills passed by the legislature are presented to the governor for his signature. They become law after being signed by the governor. State governors have item veto power. Vetoed legislation does not become a law unless it passes through the legislature by two-thirds majority vote.

The Executive Branch

Each state shall have a popularly elected Governor as its Chief Executive. The manner of election and his term and powers shall be determined by the state constitution. He shall preside over the state executive branch. It consits of the heads of the different departments which all together form the state cabinet presided by the governor. The state government is a unitary system where all governmental powers originally belong to its central government. The state subdivisions -- districts, municipalities, and villages -- receive their powers from the central government. These are delegated powers and can be extended, limited, or altered at the wish of the state legislature. Authority over the subdivisions are delegated to the Department of Interior which exercises its powers within the framework established by the state legislature. Municipalities and villages may be granted certain measures of autonomy by the state legislature.

Each state has a centralized budget system where departments, agencies, and subdivisions submit their budget proposal to a central agency under the control of the governor. One function of this agency is to improve coordination of administrative activities.

The functions of law and order is the responsibility of the National Police Department having branch offices in every state capital. In each state, this office has branches in districts, municipalities, and villages. Therefore, there is a unified national law enforcement administration. In personnel matters such as qualifications, promotion, compensation, and transfer, police officers are under the authority of the national office in Baghdad. In all functional matters relating to their duties and responsibilities, they are under the authority of their immediate chief executive. At the state level, all are under the command of the governor, at the subdivision levels they are under the authority of the district director, city mayor, or village headman. This authority extends to disciplinary actions such as suspension without pay or dismissal.

While state officials are responsible to enforce national laws and judicial dicisions, the national government may assign law enforcement officers to its branches within the state for this specific purpose only.

The benefit of this system, which is used in many countries in varying forms, is several. It requires a uniform system of education and qualifications for the position; it provides for a single national law enforcement jurisdiction. A criminal can be caught wherever he or she moves within the country. There is a uniformity in position classification and promotion. A police officer can transfer himself from one state to another or from one office to another without losing his seniority, fringe benefits and other privileges. The governors and local officials have access to a well educated and trained, and well administered police force.

In most respects the functions of the chief executive of a state -- the governor -- parallel those of the president at the national level. All have item veto power over legislation; they can approve certain parts of a bill and make them law through their signature; they can veto other parts which is returned to the legislature for reconsideration and vote. A two-thirds majority vote of the legislature is required to override the governor's veto. The item veto provides considerable discretionary power to the governor who may confine the gubernatorial veto to unfavored portions of an appropriation bill. In most cases it is quite difficult for a state legislature to raise two-thirds majority vote to override a governor's veto.

Governors also possess power to call special legislative sessions for consideration of problems that the legislature has been unable or unwilling to solve. Frequently, as experience has shown, the threat of such a special session will force a legislature to take action on a bill it has been avoiding.

The governor has a broad authority over the administrative branch of his respective state. He can reorganize the bureaucratic agencies of the state and streamline administrative methods and organizations.

In each state there is a Vice Governor who is elected with the governor on the same ticket. Other top officials are appointed by the governor subject to confirmation by the state legislature.

The Judicial Branch

Each state is a sovereign entity; it has the authority to set up whichever type of court system it sees appropriate. Since most of the controversies and offenses against society fall within the state jurisdiction under the state laws, each state needs an elaborate judicial system, the structure and functions of which shall be determined by the state constitution and the legislature. The judicial branch is independent from the other two branches of government and judges are appointed in such a manner and for such term of office to guarantee them the most possible independence from the outside forces.

Each state, by necessity, has a State Supreme Court with appellate jurisdiction and the final authority on interpretation of the state constitution and with judicial review power over state laws. In decisions relating to the rights protected by the national constitution an appeal from its decision may be taken before the Supreme Court of the United Republics. Besides the State Supreme Court the hierarchy of the state judicial system includes several courts of appeals, and local courts. The local courts consist of one judge for each court. In the case of overload of work, additional judges may be appointed. A local court may sit as a religious court in religious matters governed by the Islamic laws. All state judicial officials must be academically well acquainted with the Islamic laws and principles.

CHAPTER 8.

Fundamental Rights and Liberties

Social and Economic Foundation

National resources such as petroleum, minerals and forests, as well as basic means of production and distribution are owned by the people. Twenty percent of the proceeds from such resources goes to the state where such resource or resources are located. A major part of the rest is used by the national government to provide for universal education and health care for every citizen as prescribed by law.

The national government may contract the operation for the extraction and refinement of natural resources to the private sector for a limited but economically sound period of time. Such contracts could be renewed based on the previous efficiency and effectiveness of operation and proper public benefits.

Education is provided free of charge from pre-school, elementary and secondary levels through university and professional levels. Each state is responsible for the establishment and administration of the educational system within its territory. The education is compulsory through the secondary level. The minimum standards, quality, and curricula is established by the national law and is followed by each state. However, each state may establish its own standards, quality and content within the framework established by the national government.

There is a full preschool, elementary, secondary and higher education institutions capable of responding to the educational needs of the state population.

Preschool education embodies a full-time, four year program of education for children from three to seven years of age. The primary education is a full-time, four year program for children from seven to 11 years of age. The secondary education consists of a full-time, four year program for those from 11 to 15 years of age. These programs are heavily geared toward a liberal education in science, social sciences, and humanities. This type of curricula will eliminate the need for general education at post-secondary levels.

The higher education consists of two general areas of technical and professional-scientific. Technical education is a short term specialized education preparing the individual to enter the market in production of goods and services. These technical educational programs, depending on their nature, may last from a few weeks to two years.

Professional or scientific education may take at least four years and some such as doctors, psychologists, and lawyers may require more extended studies, research and internship.

For all these levels from the preschool on, teacher education needs to receive special attention. The best teachers raise the best contributors and performers. For this reason teachers are granted a high status in society with compensation accommodating and sustaining this dignified social position.

Health care is a national duty and is based on preventive health care. Establishment and financing a national health care program is a priority in spending. It is financed from the revenues produced from the natural resources, particularly petroleum. Since state governments are closer to the people, the administration of the health care programs are better taken care of by the states. It avoids much of the red tape and is more efficient.

Health is provided free of charge to all citizens and to others as prescribed by law. Each state will be responsible for the establishment and administration of the health care system within its territory within the general framework established by national law.

Thus in the areas of education and health care the authority and responsibility are shared by both national and state governments. The national government establishes minimum standards and provides for the budget and the state governments establish and carry out the basic functions as required and necessary for serving their residents.

Private ownership and individual economic liberty are guaranteed according to the law and no one can be deprived of life, liberty, and property without due process of law. Freedom of ownership and enjoyment of property cannot be allowed to result in consequences detrimental to public good and safety. The basic principles of ownership are prescribed in a way to result in the equitable distribution of wealth among the citizens.

Government has the power of eminent domain but no property can be appropriated except for reasons of public interest and after just and prompt compensation.

The maximum limit of agricultural property is prescribed by the law; the surplus will be owned temporarily by the state on behalf of the people until it is redistributed.

Inheritance is a conditional right; its upper limit will be prescribed by law from time to time as it becomes necessary. Inheritance is one of the most undemocratic elements in each society. It causes class stratification perpetuating wealth and power in a few families which in turn dominate or at least influence the political and economic system to the detriment of the society.

Since inheritance is traditionally accepted and practiced in nearly every society it might not be appropriate or practical to prohibit it outright. Particularly, inheritance is one of the pillars of the capitalistic system which creates and protects the economic elite which in turn dominates the social, political, and economic systems of the society.

To provide for a just and equitable society and to protect democracy as a substance as well as process, it becomes mandatory that a ceiling for inheritance be established. Such ceiling may be established in a manner to restrict only the very rich. It may affect only the top five percent of population. No detailed statistics are available about individual wealth in Iraq; however, in the United States if the maximum level of inheritance is set at 500,000 dollars, only a little over ten percent of the population will be affected. Ninety percent will receive full inheritance, the remaining ten percent can inherit only 500,000 dollars from the wealth and the surplus will go to a Public Consumption Fund to be spent on general welfare functions or economic development and investment. Relevant to this principle, any free transfer of property before death to avoid inheritance must be prohibited. For example, if this principle of limited inheritance is applied in the United States, in a matter of two or three decades all the powerful families that now dominate the operation of the society will diminish to the level of the rest of the society. Their powers and influences will disappear. This will be a great and essential victory for democracy. This limit for inheritance in Iraq may be properly set at $100,000 or less.

Individual Rights and Liberties

All persons born or naturalized in the United Republics of Iraq, and subject to the jurisdiction thereof, are citizens of the United Republics of Iraq and of the state wherein they reside. This provision is quite different from the highly restricted citizenship requirement established by the present laws. The Iraqi Interim Constitution does not establish requirement for citizenship except stating that the basic objective is the realization of one Arab State.[1] It states that Iraq is a part of the Arab Nation[2] composed of two principal nationalities: the Arab and the Kurdish.[3] However, it recognizes the legitimate rights of all minorities within the Iraqi territory.[4]

Every person is equal before the law as all others and without discrimination on account of race, language, social or national origin, or religion. The Interim Constitution recognizes these rights only for Iraqi citizens; it should be extended to all those within the Iraqi territory rather than only to its citizens.

Equality of opportunity being the basic principle of a democratic society, is guaranteed to all citizens and permanent residents. The ultimate application of equality of opportunity extends to all political, social, economic, and cultural spheres of life. This should be the goal of the constitution and that of the national as well as state governments. It cannot be applied outright; it needs to develop gradually without losing the sight of its ultimate goal. This is the only way toward a true democracy. If systematically applied, it can be achieved in a period of about three decades.[5] The implementation of equality of opportunity is established by appropriate laws; the ultimate resolution of the conflicts is vested on the judicial system.

Despite the fact that Islam is the official religion of the country, freedom of religion, faith and the exercise of religious rites are guaranteed as long as it is not in violation of the criminal laws, The confidentiality of communication by mail, telegram, telephone and other media is guaranteed except for consideration in criminal judicial proceedings.

Freedom of speech and press is recognized. Freedom of opinion, publication, meeting, peaceful demonstrations, formation of political parties and other groups for political or social expression, syndicates and societies are guaranteed. Exercise of these freedoms cannot be disruptive of the normal operation of the communities or create a clear and present danger to others.

An accused is presumed to be innocent until proved guilty through due process of law.[6] No person is deprived of life, liberty, or property without due process of law, and no person shall be denied the equal protection of the laws.[7]

Court sessions will be public unless they necessitate secrecy by a court decision for the protection of the rights of the accused and to guarantee a fair and impartial trial. In all cases the accused is entitled to a speedy and fair trial.

There can be no crime, nor punishment, except in conformity with the law. No penalty is imposed, except for criminal acts under the law, when they are committed.[8] No excessive bail or cruel and unusual punishment are allowed.[9]

No person can be arrested, stopped, imprisoned, or searched except through due process of law.[10] The right of the people to be secure in their person, houses, papers and effects is not violated except when a warrant is issued by a judge based on probable cause. Such warrant must describe the place to be searched and the persons or things to be seized.

The State undertakes the struggle against illiteracy and guarantees the right to education, free of charge, in its preschool, primary, secondary vocational and university levels, for all citizens.[11]

The National and State governments shall strive to make the primary and secondary education compulsory, to expand vocational and technical education in cities and rural areas and to encourage particularly night education enabling popular masses to combine knowledge with work.[12]

The National Government and the States shall guarantee the freedom of scientific research and reward excellence in creativity and initiative in all social, economic, cultural, historical, and technological spheres.[13]

The education shall have the objective of raising and developing the general education level, promoting scientific thinking, enlivening the research spirit, responding to exigencies of economic and social evolution and development programs, creating a liberal and progressive generation, strong physically and morally, proud of its people, its homeland and heritage, aware of all its individual and national rights based on the constitutional principle of equality of opportunity, becoming conscious of the destructive effect of social and economic exploitation and discrimination on account of race, color, sex, religion, and national origin.

Public officers are the servants of the people and the public office is a sacred confidence and social service; its essence is the honest and conscious obligation to the interests of the masses, their rights and liberties, within the framework of the Constitution as promulgated by appropriate laws. Equality of opportunity extends also to the appointments for public offices.

The defense of the homeland is a sacred duty and honor for the citizens; conscription shall be compulsory and regulated by law.[14]

Armed forces belong to the people and are entrusted with ensuring their security, defending their independence, protecting their safety and integrity and territory.[15]

The armed forces shall be under the authority of the National Government. As Commander-in-Chief the President of the United Republics shall command the armed forces following the policies and directions established by the national legislative branch.

Work is an individual right. The national and state governments shall provide means of its availability to every able citizen to the extent that each family shall have at least one bread winner.

Work is an honor and a sacred duty and responsibility for every able citizen; it is indispensable by the necessity to participate in building the society, protecting it and realizing its evolution and prosperity.

The national and state governments shall undertake to improve the conditions of work and raise the standards of living, experience and culture for all working people.

The national government in cooperation with the state governments shall undertake to provide the largest possible scale of social security for all citizens in the case of sickness, disability, unemployment or old age.

The national government in cooperation with the state governments shall assume the responsibility to safeguard the public health by continually expanding free medical services, in prevention, treatment, and medicine, expanding them to all cities and rural areas. The funds to implement all the social welfare services come primarily from the petroleum revenues with a long range, 20 year, socioeconomic development program toward bringing Iraq to the level of a highly educated conscious, self-sufficient democratic model. Iraq, with only 18 million population and great natural resources, has the means and opportunity to become a model of true democratic socialism.

Payment of taxes is the duty of everyone living within the United Republics. Both the national and state governments have authority to levy taxes for governmental expenditures and necessary public services. No tax can be imposed, modified, or levied except as prescribed by the law.

Acts detrimental to national unity are prohibited. Any act adversely affecting national unity and harmony, or provoking racial, sectarian, ethnic or religious discrimination is punishable as prescribed by the law.

The national and state legislatures have power to enforce the provisions of this constitution by appropriate legislation.

The national courts have power to interpret the Constitution, the final authority being vested on the Supreme Court of the United Republics.

State courts in each Republic have the power to interpret the state's constitution, the final authority being vested on the State Supreme Court.

In the case of conflict with national constitution the National Supreme Court has power to review the decisions rendered by a State Supreme Court.

The National Legislature, whenever two-thirds of both houses deem it necessary, proposes amendments to the Constitution which becomes part of the Constitution when ratified by the legislatures of five of the six states and District of Baghdad combined. The amendment must be ratified within the time limit prescribed by the national legislature and no state once ratified can rescind an amendment. Neither the President of the United Republics nor the state governors can veto an amendment. The National Legislature may extend the time limit for ratification if deemed appropriate.

The form of government proposed for Iraq is not based on capitalistic operation of economy. No true democracy can co-exist with a capitalistic economy since every major characteristic of the latter is undemocratic such as exploitation of workers and consumers, discrimination, induciveness to economic, social, and political corruption and abuse of power. The study of the economic system in the United States and its so-called representative democracy will illustrate the validity of this statement.

The appropriation of profit, the very concept of profit, is undemocratic since it materializes either by exploitation of labor or exploitation of consumers. Corruption and moral decay are the natural outcome of a capitalistic economy. Consider the savings and loans fiasco in the United States which is costing hundreds of billions of dollars to the taxpayers. Why did it happen? Because the government relaxed the controlling regulation allowing capitalism to show its monstrous face with vast array of embezzlements, frauds, deceits and thefts of public and private assets. Capitalism encourages deception and abuse in nearly every facet of economic life. The abuse of welfare programs by millions of individuals is a good example. Millions receive welfare payments who are not actually qualified and many are quite well-to-do. It creates welfare queens. Millions abuse the food stamp program and millions abuse medicaid programs by transferring their assets to others and making themselves technically poor in order to become qualified for the benefits of the program. According to one study this item alone costs the taxpayers over 35 billion dollars a year. It is not difficult to find hundreds of similar examples by studying reports relating to only the past three decades in the United States.

This kind of widespread corruption and drive for profits extend its effect to social and moral fabrics of the society. It substantially expands crimes and in fact encourages them. Most of this comes from the fact that capitalism creates a highly stratified society with a small economic elite at the top that governs or strongly influences the social, economic, and political operation of the society,[16] and tens of millions of poor and destitute at the bottom. These are left out of the mainstream of society and must survive on their own, often obliged to resort to illegal and criminal means. In short, capitalism is destructive of democracy. Not only does it cause inhuman behavior within the United States but it extends its cruel hands to other less developed countries to protect its interest and its expansion. Any resistance to the concept creates ferocious response dewastating societies and destroying millions of innocent lives. The Granada invasion, the Vietnam War, Operation Desert Storm, the animosity towards the Iranian regime, are just a few recent examples.

Based on these undemocratic facts of capitalistic life, the system of government proposed for Iraq is a from of democratic socialism leading the Iraqi society gradually toward a true democracy that the author has elaborated in detail in his two publications, *Technological Democracy* (1990), and *Technodemocratic Economic Theory* (1991).[17]

Democratic socialism does not eliminate capitalism but tends to minimize its effect with the expectation to eliminate it and its corresponding evils as it proceeds toward a full democracy. Under this system there is a long range national plan for democracy. First democratic goals are established. The most important and essential of those goals is the attainment of equality of opportunity in all social, economic, and political aspects of the societal life. This being the goal, there are processes embodied in the plan to start and move toward achieving this goal.

From the social viewpoint, equality of opportunity requires that education and health care are accessible the same to every citizen. This goal can be achieved only when all these services are available to everyone free of charge, namely free of any financial burden.

The principle of equality of opportunity also requires suitable old-age benefits to everyone. Initially, under a socialistic democracy, all these services will be provided for the people by the government through the use of revenues from natural resources. Gradually, as the system moves toward democracy, the burden will shift away from the government to the people. In the advanced stages of democracy, all these functions are taken away from the government and are shifted to the private sector. The size as well as the functions of the government, the national government in particular, are sharply diminished.

From the economic viewpoint, the working class is organized on the basis of merit depending on the extent of education and experience. All positions are classified by the government on this basis and the corresponding pay system is allocated for comparable classes of positions. Workers, whether employed by the government or the private sector, are employed and paid according to this classification. This is a giant step toward eliminating discrimination in the workplace. Each worker is assigned a job according to his or her merits and receives the corresponding compensation. As the society advances in the democratic process this function of position classification is gradually transferred to the production institutions, the national government responsible to establish its general framework only and the production organizations each become responsible to establish its own position classification and pay system within the general framework prescribed and periodically revised by the national government.

Besides the equal pay for similar positions and the universal merit system in employment, the principle of equality of opportunity requires the total ownership of the means of production and distribution by the individuals which form the private sector. To achieve this, each worker receives, in addition to salary, certain shares of the production institution where he or she works. As a matter of time the production capital is transferred from the capitalist in the private sector and from the governments to the working class and the era of capitalism reaches its end.

Thus, democratic socialism is the initial stage toward a full democracy. It may take a few decades for Iraqi people to travel this road. But to be able to do so, they must establish the ground which would facilitate and encourage progress toward such democracy. The type of government based on the rights and processes proposed in this writing is designed for achieving this purpose. For this reason and for attaining equality of opportunity, which will lead toward a free and prosperous society,it is imperative that the constitutional provisions proposed here be fully adopted and implemented in good faith.

Political democracy which has been around for over two centuries is no longer satisfactory in the modern technological society. Its establishment was aided by the capitalist class in the 18th century to guarantee the permanency of property rights and ownership. Since the beginning, it has been the tool of the capitalist elite for better accumulation of wealth and power. Capitalistic norms have continually influenced and often dominated the essence and operation of political democracy. As a result, today political democracy has become a facade and appearance. Dominated by the economic elite and their giant economic organizations, political democracy has become a major tool for maintaining and serving capitalistic objectives.

In recent years, however, through the advanced and global electronic information-communications systems the lower classes of the Western societies have become increasingly aware of the injustices caused by capitalism. Capitalistic exploitation, alienation, and deprivation has affected the opportunities of over 80 percent of the population, depriving them from equal opportunity to pursue life, liberty, property, and happiness. Political democracy as a servant of capitalism, has been the main cause of these socioeconomic injustices.

The presently increasing consciousness is leading to the understanding that political democracy in the absence of economic democracy not only is a useless tool but has worked against the welfare of the overwhelming majority of the people. This consciousness has led to new demands based on equality of opportunity in social and economic spheres of life.

Today, people want universal education where every citizen could have equal opportunity of access to it at all levels. People also want the transformation of the content as well as process of education in a manner to fit the rapidly changing socioeconomic conditions under the effect of everchanging technological means and processes.[18]

Today, people want health care for all. A kind of health care program which will take care of all citizens regardless of an individual's economic condition. Simply, people want equal opportunity of access to healthcare.[19]

Today, working people want to receive just compensation for their work. They want equal opportunity in the production process namely elimination of exploitation, alienation, racism, and sexism.[20] An essential progress toward this purpose is considered to be the workers participation in capital by granting each worker a gradual ownership of capital presently owned by the capitalistic class.[21]

Today, workers want a guaranteed retirement benefits, a kind that will give them comparable standing with the capitalist class. If a worker receives a share of capital each month along with his wage, he will be able to accumulate enough capital by the time of retirement from return of which he can sustain a comfortable and dignified life. There will be no need for social security programs or many other humiliating welfare programs. Today, an ordinary worker is not satisfied just by making a living but aspires for and desires a more comfortable and luxurious life. This tendency has been also mainly the effect of advanced electronic informatio-communication technology which demonstrates the way rich people live and how the workers, who bring wealth and power to the elite, are deprived of the many fruits of their own labor. This is another aspect of the rising expectations.[22]

There is no doubt that the advanced global information-communication technology has been the main cause of this enormous rise in expectations, not only within the United States but, more seriously, among the Third World countries. Most of these nations are extremely poor and less developed and are exploited by the elite countries led by the United States.[23]

High technology has sharpened class contradiction far beyond Karl Marx's imagination in his theory of communism. There is an analogy between *laissez-faire* free enterprise capitalism of a century ago and *laissez-innover* technology or the concept of free use of technological innovation of the present time.[24] Laissez-innover does not function for the benefit of mankind or society. It is primarily for the benefit of those few who control it and use it. In their technological innovations they are primarily concerned with self-benefit and try to solve the associated problems only when such problems affect them directly. The societal benefits, if any, are usually marginal.

Thus, technological elite which is under the control of the capitalist elite are not concerned with the use of technology to resolve major socioeconomic problems. They use technology where it can receive profit from it. Crucial problems of technological society such as slums in core cities, contaminated air and water, toxic waste, health care, and education are not paid due attention. These can be solved only by the proper use of technological means and processes. But, there are no tangible profits to the owners of technologies from these activities. In these respects, the elite consists of the disinterested characters of the technological decision-makers concerned primarily with benefit to themselves.

The laissez-faire capitalism during the 18th and 19th centuries, on the one hand caused rapid accumulation of capital and development of monopolies; and on the other hand, through development in information technology, it caused the destruction of the gap in political culture between the masses of population and the ruling class. This gave rise to democratic ethos and demands. The developments in printing and the postal system, brought about public access to newspapers, books and periodicals causing a general popular literacy. As a result, the organized means of popular expression brought individual literacy and social rationality to lower classes.[25] The spread of egalitarian ideas fortified the concept of popular sovereignty and establishment of representative systems.

The cycle is being repeated now as a result of the freedom of technological innovation, or dominance of laissez-innover. The dominance of technology since World War II has contributed to the erosion of those democratic ethos gained during the last two centuries by creating another class structure and growing separation between the ruling class and the rest of society. There has been a sharp decline in popular literacy in relation to understanding of the political, social and economic character of the modern technology. This ignorance reveals itself as technology penetrates the language. Ordinary people, even those otherwise well educated, cannot understand technical and technological terms entered daily into the language. These words are alien to an ordinary person.

Technology has also contributed to the growth of social irrationality. The high-tech managerial process is seen as an inalienable right of the national elite. Mystification around technology's managers has created more class isolation. The normal life of the middle and lower classes appears cut off from those experiences of the elite. The technological rationality of today is as socially neutral as the market rationality was a century ago. Both caused widening separation between the two classes of the rulers and workers. Of course, there is a sharp difference in definition of the working class under laissez-faire economy of a century ago and that of today under laissez-innover. The former consisted of mainly blue collar workers, the latter includes any working person including professionals such as lawyers, engineers and physicians.

These are very profound social contradictions, sharper and more fundamental than those assumed under a laissez-faire capitalism. Technological society requires ever more socially disciplined population, but because of technological illiteracy it retains ever declining capacity to enforce the required discipline.

The very essential detriment to society is the control of technology as well as the corresponding technological elite by the capitalist elite. Thus, as profit motives under old capitalism concentrated the control of power and wealth in the small class of capitalist elite, the same motive has caused and continues to cause the concentration of technology, a much stronger instrument of power and wealth, in the hands of the same economic elite. Technological managers serve and work for this elite. The United States society is rapidly moving toward a horrible dictatorship. It will be horrible because it will operate under the facade of political democracy. Actually the system will be under a strict elite rule through the use of high-tech information-communications media and complex organization technology,

Politically, socially, and economically there is a profound contradiction between the highly stratified society on the one hand and the spread of educational opportunity and easy access to information on the other. Thus, technology is creating the basis for a new and sharp class conflict in the society. The technological process has become the most powerful and influential element in regard to the demands and programs of the technological impulse. It identifies and rationalizes the interests of the most authoritarian elites within the United States and other technological societies.

The very essential step toward democracy in modern society consists of democratization of technological means through providing for every citizen the equality of opportunity of access to its use. Under the present control of technology by the capitalist elite, national consciousness and general strike are the clues for transformation from technological autocracy to technological democracy.

This is just a brief direction and warning to the national and state governments in Iraq. All Third World countries are affected by modern technology nearly in every aspect of societal life. The conscious and proper use of technology is utmost important to accomplish democracy. Its use must be based on the principle of equality of opportunity. The initial governmental regulation must be geared toward future democratization of the information-communication technology, even though under a social-democratic system it may be controlled by the government.

To become acquainted with the concept of democracy referred to in this chapter, the next chapter is appropriated for the scientific definition of this concept in a more general and simple form. Though this is a futuristic concept of democracy, the form, structure, and functions of the new democracy in Iraq will have direct relevance to whether or not the system will easily and steadily move toward technological democracy with equality of opportunity developed and applied to every facet of daily life.

CHAPTER 9.

DEMOCRACY DEFINED: A FUTURISTIC PERSPECTIVE

The proposed form of democratic socialism for Iraq if properly adopted and executed, will more likely lead toward a true democracy. It will also serve as a model for some other developing countries. A definition of a real democracy seems here to be in order to be used as reference and an objective for the future of the societies that strive for a democratic life.

Today, there are two general concepts of democracy.   One is *democratic capitalism*, which recognizes the need for some state regulatory activity in economic affairs but emphasizes the primacy of individual economic freedom; it presents a conservative defense of the freedom of enterprise.   The other is *democratic socialism* which emphasizes the need for radical socioeconomic reconstruction, greater range of community or state control, and the cooperative determination of planned economic objectives.

An example of democratic capitalism is the United States, where the political democratic process is used to provide justification for sustaining socioeconomic discrimination and exploitation inherent in capitalism.   An incomplete example of democratic socialism is Sweden where political democracy is attempted to maintain the unstable combination of state and private capitalism. On the other extreme, stands China where so called "democratic centralism" has been made a facade to justify state socialism. In none of these systems has a substantive democracy been materialized. It cannot materialize. What then, is democracy?

In reality, democracy as an ideology has no relevancy to capitalism or socialism; it is incompatible with both. Democracy is an independent system by itself, of which political democracy is just a part. It embodies its own political, social, and economic components. Democracy is a societal system encompassing the intricateness of society as a whole. As such, democracy has never been defined. This type of democracy cannot occur in any society which is not highly developed and broadly educated. It requires a kind of socialization where people understand the democratic principles governing all aspects of the society -- socioeconomic, political, as well as technological.

In a democratic system, political norms and processes cannot be considered in isolation from social, economic and technological norms. Democracy can be materialized when it embraces all interactions in society.

There are two parts to such a *democratic system*. The first relates to the objectives to be achieved or *substantive democracy*. The second concerns the way to go about to achieve these democratic goals. This is called *procedural democracy* or democratic process.

Substantive Democracy

There are three objectives to democracy: *Equality of opportunity* from social, economic, political and technological viewpoints; *freedom*, and *individualism*. From all these objectives, equality of opportunity is the most essential. The other two objectives -- freedom and individualism -- are mainly the result of the achievement of the first.

Freedom as envisioned here has two components: freedom to choose and freedom to act upon the choice. Often people think they have freedom of choice, but if one has no freedom to act upon the choice then that freedom is no more than an illusion. When there is an equality of opportunity then individuals who make a choice will have equal opportunity to act upon their choice. The boundaries of freedom become boundless. This will be made clear when the effect of equality of opportunity in procedural democracy is discussed.

Individualism is also mainly an outcome of the application of the principle of equality of opportunity. It means that in a democratic society the individual is the measure of value. Operation of society is based on and is for ascertaining individual dignity, desire, aspiration and demands. The individual has socioeconomic security and is important as an indispensable component of the democratic system. Figure 9-1 illustrates the system.

Procedural Democracy

Procedural democracy is the operational aspect of democracy. It is a process which is designed to lead the society toward attaining substantive democracy by achieving democratic objectives.

Procedural democracy has three components: political, socioeconomic, and technological. Here we will discuss the first two. Technological democracy as an indispensable part of democracy. As technology advances, its effects on the democratic process increases. It becomes a highly dominant factor in the highly developed societies. We exclude the eminence of technology in our discussion of democracy here because we are primarily concerned with the application of democracy in less developed countries. By no means does this exclusion reduce the effect of technology in the democratic process in these countries. Today, in most of the developing countries people have access to television, radio, newspapers and magazines. Through the satellite system people also have access to what is going on in other parts of the world. For the democratic process in developing countries the principle of equality of opportunity should also apply to the use of technology at least in the political process.

Political Procedural Democracy

The objective is to apply the principle of equality of opportunity in every aspect of the political process toward achieving political democracy. There are three requirements to establish political procedural democracy: popular sovereignty, majority rule with

Figure 9-1. Components of Technological Democracy

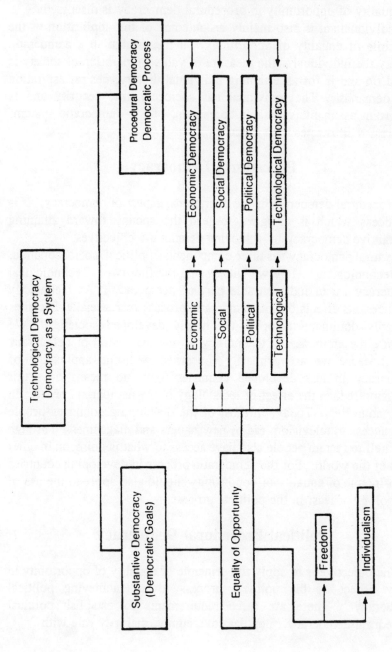

minority rights and limited government. Figure 9-2 illustrates the process.

Popular sovereignty is achieved when people as a whole have full authority over the government. This is possible only when there is a free and frequent election. There are at least six requirements for free elections: equality of opportunity in electing and being elected, in financial requirements, information, expression, and in organization for political purposes.

In the United States, though nearly every eligible person can vote, candidates are selected and supported by the elite and voters are manipulated through media and other campaign instruments to vote for them. Thus in reality there is no equality of opportunity to elect or be elected.

For free elections there should also be equality of opportunity in the financial aspects of the electoral process. For example, in the United States, money is the lifeblood of elections, therefore, there is no free election.

Equality of opportunity of access to information is another requirement for free elections. Information is vital for evaluating and selecting proper policies and representatives. When the sources and means of information is owned or controlled by an elite, the information will be screened, edited, or manipulated to protect the interest of those who control it. Consequently, voters will not have equal opportunity of access to information and free elections will be hampered. Again the United States is a good example.[1]

Finally, free elections require that the voters have equal opportunity to express themselves and organize for political purposes. Permanent political parties deprive nonmembers from the equal opportunity to express themselves or organize for that purpose. Political organizations must be temporary in order to avoid institutionalization for power and influence. The long established two party system in the United States is a good example of creating an unequal atmosphere in the political process detrimental to the majority of the voters.[2]

The second requirement of political procedural democracy is the *majority rule with minority rights*. Majority rule alone may not guarantee democratic process, it may end in *majority dictatorship* which is the worst kind of dictatorship since it is a dictatorship with the appearance of democracy. Majority rule must accompany minority

Figure 9-2 Prerequisites of Political Equality of Opportunity

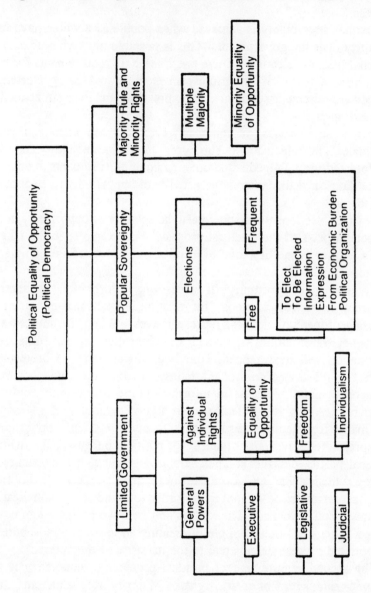

rights where the minority is given equal opportunity with the majority in participation, debate, expression, organization and voting.

The third requirement is *limited government*. The application of the principle of equality of opportunity limits powers of government in two ways. First, in the area of general powers, namely legislative, executive, and judicial. The requirement of equality of opportunity places the public authorities and the citizens at the same level. The government has the least interference with the daily affairs of individuals, and individuals have access to all government archives, information, and functioning. In democratic society the size of government is minimal and its functions highly restricted. Second, the government is limited in the area of individual rights. These rights are strictly governed by the principle of equality of opportunity and thus protected by it. It leaves little room for the government to interfere with the proper exercise of these rights.

Socio-Economic Procedural Democracy

The attainment of socioeconomic democracy depends on the implementation of socioeconomic equality of opportunity. To achieve this goal there is a need for economic procedural democracy, based on the principle of equality of opportunity. It requires two prerequisites: prohibition of unjust enrichment and shared opportunity. It requires the application of the principle of equality of opportunity in four areas of capital, labor, state, and technology. Figure 9-3 illustrates the situation. Economic democracy is central to the attainment of a democratic society. There cannot be any kind of real democracy without achieving first the economic democracy. Here we deal with the first three areas leaving out the discussion of technology.

A. Capital

To democratize the ownership of capital, the principle of equality of opportunity requires the prohibition of unjust enrichment. Unjust enrichment simply means that no one receives property or services without giving in return a compensation comparable in value. The prohibition of unjust enrichment causes the following consequences in the economic operation of society.

Figure 9-3. **Prerequisites of Economic Equality of Opportunity**

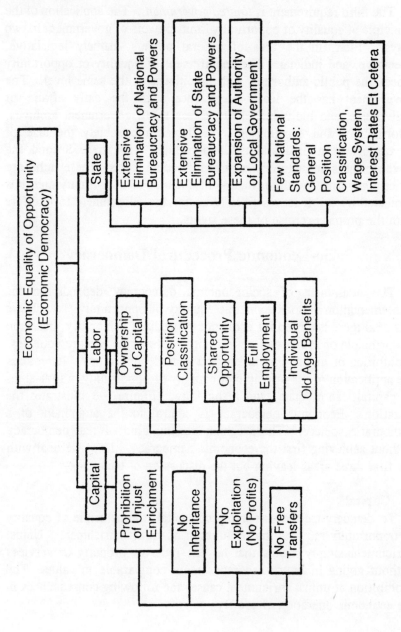

1.   Limited Inheritance.   Since anything received through inheritance is free and without comparable compensation, therefore, it is unjust enrichment and thus must be prohibited.   Inheritance, to the extent of wealth received, elevates the opportunity of the beneficiary to the detriment of others.   In capitalistic societies, it has been the most important cause of creating unequal opportunities, not only in the economic but also extending it to social and political areas.   It has created the economic elite in these countries dominating all aspects of the life in society.[3]

The proceeds from inheritance will go into a Public Consumption Fund which will be spent in providing vital services such as education and health care.   The result is that as the rich individuals die, their wealth instead of going to their heirs, is transferred to the public treasury and spent for the public good.   The consequence of this practice is that gradually wealthy families, which enjoyed a very high opportunity under capitalism, will disappear while their riches are used to enrich and enlighten the masses as a whole.   In a span of a few decades, society will cease to have any multi-millionaires.   The ruling capitalist elite will die and with it will disappear its dominating socioeconomic and political powers.

In a democratic society inheritance may be allowed to the extent that it will not disturb or contradict with the principle of equality of opportunity.   This can occur only when every individual in society receives the same amount of inheritance.   This limit is determined by the minimum amount of wealth left at the death of individuals divided by the maximum size of the family.   This amount is determined periodically from the national statistics.   For example, if this minimum amount was $20,000, then everyone will be allowed to inherit that amount.   Since inheritance to this extent will not disturb the equality of opportunity, its exercise will be democratic.   This level of inheritance will have its other benefits as well.   For example, individuals will have opportunity to possess the personal effects of their parents or some other items relating to the family or having particular sentimental values.

As the society advances toward the full state of democracy, the amount of family wealth will tend toward general equalization.   Accordingly, the amount of wealth left by most of the individuals, though not exactly the same, will be at the same level with some variations.

Figure 9-4 illustrates the development of allowable inheritance and the disappearance of very rich as a matter of time. Here the estimated time for this development is 60 years from the time of the establishment of the limited inheritance. During this period nearly all multi-millionaires will die and except for the negligible amount allowed for inheritance, their wealth will be transferred to the Public Consumption Fund. As illustrated in Figure 9-4, during the first ten years the allowable inheritance will be near zero and during the second decade it may amount only to a few thousand of dollars.

In a capitalistic society like the United States it may be appropriate to take a moderate method to achieve this goal. Though generally people are in favor of inheritance, they are annoyed by the transfer of tens or hundreds of millions of dollars down some family line from generation to generation perpetuating its socioeconomic and political power to the substantial detriment of the rest of society. People, more likely will support a cap on inheritance as long as it affects only a small minority of the rich households.

For example, if the maximum level of inheritance was established at 600,000 dollars per household, it will affect only about ten percent of the households. More likely such restriction will receive the approval of 70-90 percent of the American households with the estimated assets of $600,000 or less. There are three reasons for such massive support of this limitation on inheritance. First, it will tend to eliminate, and ultimately will eliminate the economic elite and with it its socioeconomic and political powers. Second, it provides for substantial amounts of funds to be spent on education and health care benefiting equally the whole society. Third, there will be no inheritance tax which will benefit the whole 90 percent of households.

As a matter of time, as illustrated in Figure 9-4, the wealth of the capitalist elite will diminish leading toward equalization with the rest of society. There will be a few which may accumulate substantial but not enormous amounts of wealth. This will be of no problem since the ownership will expire with the death of the owner.

The result of application of the original method will be that the minimum wealth at the time of death will substantially increase reaching the equalized wealth of the estimated $600,000 within six decades. This will necessarily increase the level of allowable inheritance. The minimum allowable inheritance is determined on the basis of the family size. For example, if the wealth left is $400,000

Figure 9-4. The Effect of Limited Inheritance

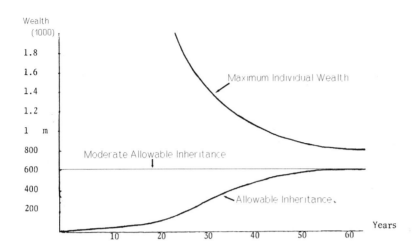

and the largest family size is four, then the allowable inheritance for the whole nation will be $100,000 per person.

If inheritance is allowed in a democratic society, it will apply only to the immediate members of the family such as husband, wife, and children. It must be noted that the effects of inheritance is temporary and nonaccumulative. When the receiver dies, all reverts to the public consumption fund. The heirs, if any, receive the minimum allowable from the total wealth of the deceased.

2. No Profits. As democratic economy takes over, profits will be automatically eliminated. Profits materialize from two sources:

a. Through exploitation of workers. The capitalist appropriates to himself part of labor's work without compensation, hence unjustly enriching himself. If profits are eliminated, workers will receive the full benefit of their work. When the workers become also the owners, the profits ensuing from exploitation will be automatically eliminated. They will revert to the workers as capital in the form of stocks of the production institution.

b. Through exploitation of consumers. If the capitalist charges a price which is above the full cost of production, then he exploits the consumer to the extent of the price surplus. Both exploitation of the workers as well as the consumer is unjust enrichment and thus prohibited. Both adversely affect the equality of opportunity. With the advancement of democratic economy, the exploitation of consumers will be ultimately and automatically eliminated.

It has been said that if profits are eliminated, there will be no incentive to work. Nothing can be further from the truth regarding this claim. In the first place, workers were those who worked and not the capitalist. Secondly, if the worker receives full return for his work, in contrast to partial return he received under the capitalist system, he will have far more incentive to work than before. It must be noted that in advanced democratic society, the term worker applies to any working person within the productive system, from unskilled workers up to top managers.

3. No transfer of property without just compensation. Any transfer of property without just compensation moves its receiver to a higher level of opportunity producing unjust enrichment. Thus, for the sake of democracy and maintaining equality of opportunity, it must be prohibited. Certain minor gift items may be excluded from this rule.

B. Labor

There is a very basic distinction between capitalism and democratic economy. Under capitalism the capitalist controls land, capital and technology, and employs labor from the market. Under democratic economy the workers own and control the capital and all other means of production. Generally speaking, it can be said that all labor is collectively self-employed.

1. Ownership of capital. The principle of equality of opportunity controls the process of ownership of capital. It is through this principle that the ownership of capital is democratized, materializing the total private ownership of the means of production and distributions by the working class to the extent never achieved before.

The process of achieving this goal prescribes that the ownership of capital be gradually and systematically transferred from the capitalist to the workers. For this purpose while each worker receives a regular wage, he also receives with it a certain amount of the shares of the firm where he works. Thus, from the time he receives his first pay, he starts to become a part owner of his firm. As the years pass, the worker continues to accumulate capital and increase his share of ownership. As the big capitalists die, their share of stocks revert to the public treasury and from there are offered to the stockmarket for sale. These are purchased by different institutions, public institutions in particular, and gradually transferred to the workers along with their monthly pay. Figure 9-5 illustrates this process of transfer.

After a few decades, the capitalist class as we know today, disappears and the ownership as well as control of capital becomes wholly transferred to the workers.

From there on as the retired workers die, their share of stocks go to the public treasury, from there to the stock market and finally purchased by different institutions and gradually divided among the new generation of workers along with their pay. The worker receives cash pay, which is intended to take care of his and his family's living expenses. He also receives a share of stocks, which helps him to save and accumulate capital.

Capital will still be one of the important forces of production but different from its counterpart in a capitalistic or socialistic system. In a capitalistic system the accumulation is through appropriation of the social surplus (profits from the workers) and added surplus (profits from consumers) through exploitation of labor and consumers. In a socialistic society the accumulation is the result of exploitation of labor through forced appropriation of the proceeds of production by the government.

In a society under democratic economy the accumulation of capital is direct result of savings by the labor force. These savings are the result of surpluses left after each individual laborer spends his earnings to satisfy his and his family's needs. Simply, the accumulated capital is not the result of any kind of exploitive process but the outcome of labor's own work. Returns from its use also is not through exploitation. Furthermore, its ownership ends by the death of its owner. There is no continuing accumulative system since no accumulation extends beyond the owner's life.

We must note that there is a very important distinction between the capital accumulated under a capitalist system and the one accumulated under a democratic economy. The former is the result of the appropriation by the capitalist of the profits materialized through the exploitation of labor. This is, therefore, an *unfair accumulation* forming a *malignant capital* which tends to empower the capitalists further and subjects the workers to more exploitation. Whereas, the capital accumulated under democratic economy is through savings by

Figure 9-5. Transfer of Capital and Profits to Workers

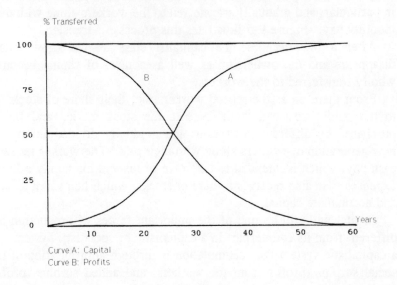

Curve A: Capital
Curve B: Profits

the worker from his earnings.[4] It is a *fair accumulation* forming a *beneficial capital* which causes more prosperity and employment opportunity for the working class and provides income and security for their old age after retirement.

Therefore, since the capital accumulated by the workers, as a result of their own labor, is a "beneficial capital," it is justified if it receives reasonable returns from its investment which will directly benefit the individual worker holding the capital. First, the capital would be loaned for which the owner receives a fixed rate of return similar to interest rate under capitalism. Second, it could be invested, for which the investor receives shares of ownership of the firm at the market price. Returns from such accumulation could be used for the purpose of providing for more comfortable living conditions, could be saved for a better life after retirement, or could be reinvested.

Each worker also has another automatically accumulating capital through the shares of ownership he receives each month along with his wage. The owner receives full benefits of ownership of these shares except that this capital cannot be transferred or sold. It can be exchanged in the stock market with other nontransferable stocks. This capital accumulates and remains intact until the owner dies. It then reverts to society to be used in the same way by the new generation. The philosophy behind this is that this capital is for the old age security of the worker, income from which will support him during this period. It is a kind of social security fund held by the individual worker rather than by the government. There is no social security program under democratic economic system. All these rules are scientifically reached by the application of the principle of equality of opportunity.

Working Class Under Democratic Economy

A very important aspect of the democratic economic theory is that it eradicates the gap between the capitalist and working classes. It eliminates distinction between these two classes and gradually molds them into one. For the first time in modern production history, the worker becomes involved in the whole process of production. He has input as to what is going to be produced, how it is going to be produced, and what is going to be done with the product after it is produced. Alienation of labor, a major cause of social contradiction and struggle of masses, is eliminated.

This new democratic mode of production is attained by the application of the principle of equality of opportunity. First, the principle does not allow any kind of exploitation, which is presently practiced under the capitalist and socialist mode of production. By its very nature, exploitation of any kind increases the opportunity of its beneficiary to the detriment of the exploited. Thus, a continuous exploitation causes a continuous rise in the level of opportunity of the beneficiary, ever widening the gap between the level of opportunities of the exploiting and exploited classes.

To eliminate this exploitation the worker must receive full compensation for his work. This means that after the worker is compensated, there will be no social surplus left for the capitalist to benefit in the form of profits.

Second, there is no equality of opportunity when the form and process of production is decided without input from the part of the workers, and when without their participation in policy conception and formulation, they are forced to produce products they did not consent to its production. This, however, does not mean that in democratic economic system all the workers in an institution should collectively participate and make decisions as to what they want to produce and how they want it to be produced. It simply means that these two decisions must be made by appropriate and qualified representatives of the workers who are also part owners of the capital of the firm.

In analyzing these situations we must bear in mind that equality of opportunity is not an abstract principle. As we have explained before, it is a principle subject to relativity, based on reason and reasonableness. Opportunities can be expected to be near exactly equal when the qualifications of two persons are exactly the same, including their intelligence, education and experience. This will be a rare case, if possible at all. Therefore, the equality of opportunity is judged, taking into consideration all productive qualities of the individuals with reasonable evaluation and nearest proximation.

Opportunity levels are of two kinds: *Initial* and *Gained*. The initial opportunity level is based on each individual's natural competence, without counting the effect of outside factors such as education and experience. From this viewpoint, the opportunity level for each individual is different from the other. This level is determined by the level of mental and physical capabilities of each individual at the time of birth. Thus, individuals are not born with equal opportunities. As they enter the world and face outside factors, educational opportunities in particular, and as by these contacts, they increase their knowledge, and thus competence, they reach a high level of opportunity. This is a stage of gained opportunity. Therefore, even if a person is born with a lower level of opportunity, he may increase the level of his opportunity through seeking knowledge and experience. This makes the availability of education and experience imperative for increasing and equalizing of the opportunity levels. If the opportunity of education and experience is available to some and not to others, then the level of opportunity of the beneficiaries will rise faster than that of others.

Though individuals start life with unequal initial opportunities they can move up their opportunities to equalize them with those with a higher initial opportunity. However, each individual has a ceiling in his level of opportunity, based on the level of his initial opportunity and intelligence. This ceiling cannot be surpassed and can be attained only by the maximum use of one's capabilities. These different opportunity ceilings among individuals establish in each society what we may call opportunity classes. The crucial point in technological democracy is that everyone within each production opportunity class should fully enjoy the equality of opportunity with others within that class.

Thus, by full availability of educational opportunities, people are able to raise their level of opportunity to the level they may desire. This attained level may not be the optimum possible for each individual since one may not desire to reach his maximum level of opportunity. This means that the opportunity for further improvement was available but the individual, with his own free will, chose not to improve it further. This tendency may not be desirable in capitalistic society, but will be quite common under democratic economic system where materialism does not dominate life, and happiness in life is not determined in material terms. Consequently, individuals are classified according to the level of opportunity they have achieved based on their education, experiences and personal desire. They form administrators, engineers, lawyers, accountants, computer scientists, technicians, economists, and different echelons of white- and blue-collar workers. Each individuals's competencies are examined and certified by an appropriate institution.   This certification determines the levels of opportunity available for each individual. Presently, there is this kind of certified classification though it is fragmented, disorganized, and often discriminatory.   For example, there are elementary and secondary school certifications, college certifications (bachelors, masters and doctoral levels) in great variety of areas and disciplines, certification in a wide variety of technical specialties, etc.

Let us see how this class system of opportunities is transferred into the production process.   In actual operation of production, opportunities have a hierarchical structure which is based on different levels of competence required to carry out a great variety of functions. There are positions for top, middle and lower level managers, professionals, technicians, specialists, skilled and unskilled workers. Each level within the individual opportunity class has a matching level of positions within the hierarchy of the production process.   The competency and performance required for each of these positions have been prescribed in detail and all the positions are classified according to the level of competency required. Presently, there are such position classifications in both capitalist and socialist societies but it is fragmented and uncoordinated with an unequal framework of formulation. For example, in the United States, we have position classifications within the national as well as state bureaucracies. Also, many business and other institutions have their own position classification system.

For open positions the individuals are examined regarding their competence which also determines their level of opportunity. It is within each level of opportunity that equality of opportunity must apply in providing positions for all those within that specific level. According to this process of application of the principle of equality of opportunity, there cannot be discrimination within each level of opportunity. Equality of opportunity in employment will apply whether the applicant is male or female, Black, or belongs to different ethnic groups or religions.

Besides initial opportunity and gained opportunity, there is also what we may call *lost opportunity*. This occurs first, when a person is deprived or denied the opportunity to raise the level of his competence and consequently raise the level of his opportunity, such as if a person is deprived of or denied the opportunity to educate himself. This is one of the characteristics of a capitalist society, like the United States, where at the lower levels of education, elementary and secondary, the poor sectors of society are provided with educational opportunities far below those of well to do and wealthy sectors. As a result, poor and minority groups are denied the chance to appropriate high quality education, depriving them from raising their level of opportunity. Second, lost opportunity occurs when a person, because of exploitation, is not granted equal opportunity in employment. Again, this is a characteristic of a capitalist society like the United States. Poor and minority groups are denied employment opportunities granted to rich and non-minority groups. Suppose individuals A and B, both college graduates with the same academic achievements, look for employment. A's father is a wealthy corporate executive; B, on the other hand, comes from a poor or a minority family. A, because of his father's connections, will have a variety of available positions to choose from. B, however, will have difficulty finding a job, and if he is finally able to find it, it may not be within his specialty or a suitable one.

Third, the lost opportunity may be the result of wage discrimination. For example, women and minority members in the

United States are paid much less than other workers for the same kind of job.

In each of these situations, when the discriminatory practice is carried out for an extended period of time, the continuous loss of opportunities widens the gap between the deprived group and the rest of the working class. It results in an undemocratic class stratification.

While lost opportunity is a major characteristic of a capitalist society, it does not exist under a democratic economic system. In the period of transition from capitalism to democratic economy, it is up to the system to see that those subjected to lost opportunities be compensated, moving them gradually to other levels of opportunity. The intention must be to close the gap between the highest and the lowest levels of opportunity. The differentiation between the opportunity levels must tend to correspond to differentiation between the levels of competence.

In this process of change, during the transition period, the differentiation in the opportunity levels for employment must be based purely on competence and experiences, and not on wealth and residually attained power and status. Once society reaches the advanced stage of technodemocratic economy, capitalists are automatically eliminated, their power and social status disappear and opportunities tend to be based strictly on competence and experience.

Shared Opportunity and Employment Right

An outcome of the principle of equality of opportunity is the right of every individual to employment. This simply means that if an individual loses his job or is not able to find employment corresponding to his level of competence, he is denied the employment opportunity that he is entitled to, while his working fellows enjoy that opportunity. Under this circumstance, there is no equality of opportunity present between those who are employed and those who are not. To remedy the situation the system must provide the unemployed individual with an appropriate employment opportunity. By an "appropriate" employment opportunity it is meant that the person must have a position corresponding to his level of competency, so that his skills and experiences could be used fully and productively, and his pay schedule corresponds to his level of opportunity.

Shared opportunity signifies a situation where there are unemployed workers and there are no open positions available for their employment. By the very fact of being unemployed with no jobs available, their opportunity has been lowered, compared to their fellow workers who are employed. To equalize these two different opportunities, and bring about equality of opportunity, the working fellows must share a small part of their employment opportunity with their unemployed fellows. For example, looking upon this issue in general at the national level, let us assume that there are ten million workers on the job and upon graduation from different educational and training institutions, an estimated 250,000 individuals enter the job market. Let us consider the extreme situation and assume also that there is no job available on the market for any of these newcomers. If this happens in a capitalist society, like the United States, all the newcomers will remain unemployed, become welfare recipients, demoralized, and a burden upon the society. Under democratic economy, if each of the working persons gives up one hour of his forty hours work per week, that is, if he works only 39 hours and receives pay for 39 hours instead of 40, there will be 10 million work hours released providing for 250,000 new positions which will accommodate all the newcomers in the job market. Sacrifice of one hour's pay would hardly affect a worker's financial situation or daily family life and obligations, while it would provide a means of livelihood for 250,000 new workers and their families. The workers who sacrifice that one hour, in actuality, do not lose all the pay for that one hour, because otherwise the government has to support 250,000 unemployed and their families through its welfare funds, available through the imposition of taxes on the working people. By using this process of "shared opportunity," the principle of equality of opportunity continues to prevail and full employment is maintained all the time. There is no need to tax working people in order to raise revenues to support millions of unemployed and their dependents. There is no lay off of workers during a sluggish market situation. By the application of the concept of shared opportunities, all the workers of a firm will remain on the job. Instead of lay offs the hours of work for each employee will be reduced with the corresponding pay. All workers will work several hours less than their full week work hours. In essence everyone will be partially laid off. For example, let us assume that a firm has 10,000 employees and has to lay off 1,000 workers or ten percent of its total work force. If instead of laying off these 1,000 workers, the firm reduces the weekly work hours by ten percent, it will not need to lay off anyone. If we assume that each worker works 40 hours per week, and the work load is reduced by ten percent, each worker will work 36 hours and will get pay for 36 instead of 40 hours. As a result, there will be no lay offs and all the workers will keep their jobs. Doing it any other way will be contrary to the principle of equality of opportunity. At the time of recession, this will resolve the most serious problems of unemployment. In financial terms, this means that billions of dollars, which otherwise had to be used for unemployment compensation and welfare payments, will now be channeled into the production process to help the economy and recovery. This self nourishing financial process, tends actually to eliminate or make highly unlikely, the occurrence of recessions or depressions. The equality of opportunity prescribes that the workers share together the good as well as the bad times.

Inflations and recessions are very unlikely under democratic economic system. Two of the main reasons for this optimism we already know. Under a democratic economic system since there is no drive for profits, prices remain quite stable and because of shared opportunities, there is always full employment. Application of the principle of shared opportunity is also eased by the fact that the workers are the owners of capital under democratic economic theory.

Position Classification and the Wage System

At every level of work hierarchy, compensation is based on the level of required competence and experience. Competence is determined by the level of education corresponding to the responsibilities of the position and experience is based on the relevant knowledge and expertise acquired through time at the work place. The general level of compensation is determined through a general position classification at the national level. The work system is divided into different classes and within each class into different levels.

There is a National Economic Council and under its authority, there is a National Position Classification Commission. As the operating tools of the system, this commission classifies all available positions provided by computerized data and establishes the level of competence and experience required for each position. This appears to be a difficult task. It is not so. Under a national computerized information system, information about all jobs in the country, and duties allocated to each, are easily collected. An assortment of the positions and classification are all carried out through this computer system and made available to the commission. Of course this national position classification does not attempt to specify in detail every available position. The classification is general, yet thorough and specific, at each level. It also establishes the general level of pay and compensation for different classes of position within each level. This is all the commission needs to do. From there on, the system of positions and compensations are updated each year; nearly all the work is done by the computer. The commission's functions will relate partially to resolution of specific problems relating to classification and wages.

Each production or service institution establishes its own position classification and pay system, according to the general classification system established by the national commission, available to it through its computer terminal. In more advanced stages of economic democracy, each institution will feed its position classification and pay system directly into the central computer. They will be checked automatically against the nationally established framework and deficiencies, if any, will be pointed out by the computer which must be corrected by the institution. These deficiencies will be electronically reported to the regional office of the National Economic Council. The most important point with this system is that while the national authorities establish a framework for position classification and pay systems, they do not go ahead and do the actual classification or assign the actual compensation for each position. All these responsibilities are transferred to the local private institutions, which are better equipped to classify them with allocations of appropriate pay for each position. Thus, the enormous bureaucratic system of doing such work at the national or regional level is eliminated by transferring the task to individual institutions.

The execution of this system is much simpler and less burdensome than the system presently used in industrial societies. Its great benefit is that it provides for equality of opportunity through a uniform system of classification and compensation, and it eliminates the bureaucracies of the present civil service commissions (national, state, and local) and similar agencies within industries and other large institutions which operate such systems. A further benefit is that it extends the scientific classification system to every production institution in society, regardless of size, including those self-employed.

Characteristics of the Pay System

With taking into consideration that pay for each position strictly corresponds to the level of competency and experience required for that position, the pay system under democratic economy has two major characteristics. First, compensation for each position consists of two parts: a cash payment which we may call a wage, and payment in stocks of the employee's firm. However, the cash payment must be sufficient to provide the worker with a convenient living condition. Projecting this minimum pay to the present economic conditions of the United States, we may dwell in the vicinity of an annual income of $14,000, or about $7.50 per hour. Presently, the minimum wage in the United States is about $4.00 per hour. This amounts to an annual earning of about $8,300 about 60 percent of our proposed minimum pay. In addition to this $14,000 minimum wage, each employee also receives a certain number of the stocks of the firm. In order to determine the amount of stock that each employee must receive, it must be taken into consideration that the accumulated amount of these stocks within thirty years of employment will be appropriate to provide a return sufficient for sustaining a convenient living condition, at least at the level of the median wage paid. One must notice here that there is no likelihood of inflationary process in democratic economy, so the value of the unit of money received will remain stable for years and more likely, for decades.

Stock allocations take place each month concurrent with the salary payment. The result is a gradual transfer of capital from capitalist to working class to the effect that, after a period of time, all capital is transferred to the workers and there is no capitalist involved in the production and distribution process.

Regarding the gradual transfer of ownership of a firm to workers, the question may arise whether there would be enough stocks of a given firm to satisfy ownership accumulation necessary for each worker to provide for a comfortable living condition after retirement.

This will be dependent on the assets-per-employee ratio in each production firm.

First, let us consider the capital adequate to have returns sufficient to provide for a comfortable living for a retired worker. Let us assume every worker to accumulate $120,000 of capital by the time of retirement and after 30 years of work. For accumulation of such capital each worker needs to receive $4,000 worth of stocks each year or $334 per month. At a seven percent return, $120,000 will produce $8,400 annual return.

Second, if we assume that the return on the capital from the beginning is also accumulated, in a period of 30 years this will amount to $140,000, which will produce an income of $9,800 at seven percent interest rate. These will give the retired worker a total annual income of $18,200. Considering that there will not be any kind of individual taxation, this amount will be equivalent, under the present conditions in the United States, to about $20,000. This will provide for comfortable living conditions, by considering the sharply reduced expenditures of life under democratic economy. First, two of the most expensive expenditures in life, namely, health care and education will be provided free of charge; second, the revolutionary process of marketing and shopping which will take place will cause substantial reduction in prices of commodities, such as goods, services, and electronic as well as live recreational programs; and third, individuals will tend toward a more simplified, though highly advanced, material life and a more intense, intellectual and spiritual one. Furthermore, in democratic society, during the retirement period, at least two people, more likely, will live together. This multiplies the combined income while reducing the expenditures.

Thirdly, it is very likely that the individual will have also personal assets accumulated from his own savings, particularly during the later years of his employment when his income surpasses his expenditures. These savings will provide for additional income which we are not considering here. It could be quite a substantial amount.

To safeguard these benefits for the retirement period the share of stocks received by the worker during his working years and returns accrued from them are not transferable. Returns from the nontransferable stocks owned by the worker are issued to him also in the form of nontransferable stocks until the time of his retirement. From there on he receives cash returns for the total of his stocks. This is a substitute for the present retirement and social security benefits except that under the democratic economy the worker has the ownership of and full benefits from his accumulated capital. He is made the trustee of his social security funds.

The assumed level of nontransferable stocks accumulation at $120,000 is based at the minimum level of assets-per-employee in the United States and other industrialized countries.[5]

Therefore, the assumption of retirement capital accumulation at the level of $120,000 is quite conservative. It will likely go far above this amount providing for much higher retirement income. At the same time it is possible that there may be a smaller number of companies where the asset per-employee ratio may be below $120,000 assumed in our retirement program. This situation may occur in certain labor incentive production firms. In such cases, in order to guarantee the capital accumulation appropriate for retirement benefits the company will be required to purchase from the free market stock of other companies with higher than average assets-per employee rate and transfer those to the workers in non-transferable fair as part of their monthly pay. At any case, this will be a marginal situation and will not affect the soundness of the retirement system. It must be noticed that monthly transfer of shares to each worker is part of his pay package and under the national position classification it applies to every worker namely a cash pay plus a share of stocks. If a worker receives cash wage but does not receive stocks, he is entitled to, then his total monthly income becomes to that extent less than the workers in other comparable positions who receive full benefit. This situation will disturb the principle of equality of opportunity, will amount to exploitation, and will endanger the retirement benefits of such worker. However, a close study of the operation of the democratic economy will disclose that this situation will be very unlikely to happen.

In order to maintain the principle of equality of opportunity as well as to safeguard the control of each firm by its workers, certain requirements are necessary:

1. Stocks in public possession will have no voting rights. Upon the death of every individual his or her holdings will go under public possession (Public Consumption Fund), until they are purchased in the open market by the corresponding firms or individuals, there always would be some stocks in the public possession. This rule is to keep the public institutions out of the production and distribution process.

2. Returns from the publicly possessed stocks will go to the Public Consumption Fund.

3. No production firm can own stocks of another firm except when they are purchased to be transferred to the workers of the firms and are kept for a short term for this purpose.

4. Candidates for the board of directors are elected from the workers of the firm. No persons from outside of the firm will be elected to any policy-making position. Top management which is not elective but appointive based on qualifications remains outside of this rule.

One of the major distinctions between the capitalist mode of production and the democratic mode of production, is that under the latter, despite a total private ownership of the means of production there is no separation between capital and labor. Labor owns the capital and thus governs the policy-making and management process, two important factors in the production process from which labor is totally detached under capitalism.

Under democratic economy each individual is the holder of his source of income for the duration of his retired life. He depends on no one for his support and is the owner of the capital accumulated, not through exploiting others but through his own labor. It is this capital that contributes to the demands of production while providing enough income for a dignified individualistic and independent life for its owner, the retired worker. However, this retirement is formal and actually the person never retires from being productive.

To protect this comfortable old age living for the workers, it is imperative that the stocks earned by each worker in addition to returns from them remain in his possession for the period of his life. For this very important purpose, these stocks and returns must be non-transferable. However, in order to diversify stock ownership, these non-transferrable stocks are exchangeable with other non-transferrable stocks available in the stock market. For example, a worker who works for company A and receives stocks of that company as part of his monthly pay, may desire to exchange part of his stocks with non-transferrable stocks of company B and C. Since many workers working for different firms would also like to diversify their non-transferrable stocks of their company, workers of company A will have no difficulty in exchanging their stocks with those of other companies in the open market. The value of non-transferrable stocks of each company is determined by the value of transferable stocks of the same company in the stock market. It must be noted that most of the stocks offered in the stock market will be of non-transferrable kind.

One may argue that since these stocks are non-transferrable, its ownership is not complete. Considering the purpose of these stocks, this argument is not valid. Because, these stocks are given to the workers, first, to transfer capital from the capitalist to the workers; second, to provide an additional source of income for the workers during their working years; third, and the most essential, to provide for a source of sufficient income for the workers after they retire. If these stocks were transferable it would have been possible for a worker to liquidate them in the market and spend the proceeds. In this way, he would have destroyed his source of maintenance during his old age. He would also have relinquished his ownership of capital. Since, under democratic economic system, there is no welfare assistance, except for those who are disabled, if such a worker liquidates his stocks, he may not have sufficient income to maintain himself. Public assistance to such a person would be contrary to the principle of equality of opportunity since by liquidating his stocks and spending the proceeds he consciously has harmed his equality of opportunity, and by receiving welfare assistance, he would be unjustifiably using the money earned by others for his support. Finally, non-transferrable stocks have all the benefits of ownership, except being transferable. The owners receive return from them and they are as valuable as transferable stocks of the same company. Furthermore, one must note that most of the investment capital will be in the form of non-transferrable stocks and thus, most of the stocks in the stock market will be of non-transferrable kind. The philosophical idea behind this is that the capital as a means of production, does not belong to anyone, but to society as a whole. Each person during his lifetime becomes the custodian of some of it and enjoys the benefits accrued from it. When the person dies, since there is no inheritance under democratic economy, the capital he owns is transferred to the public treasury and gradually passed on to the next generation. Non-transferrablility of the stocks guarantees to every worker a share of ownership of capital, it materializes the equitable distribution of the means of production and distribution among all the members of the working class.

The Work System

Under democratic economy, there is a general education program which every individual is required to complete. This general education is somehow similar in its structure, but not in its content, to the system of general education presently applied in the socialist countries like Russia. It consists of a four-year preschool education (age three through six), a four-year elementary education, and a four-year secondary education. We consider these grades one through 12. This is the most important part of each individual's education and enormously effective in the future competence of the work force.

Work starts at the age of 15. However, the individual works only part-time. There are two sides to a worker's life. First, his development as a human being necessary to prepare him as a conscious participant in a democratic society. Here the purpose of worker's education is to develop and advance him as a *democratic person*. Such a person is deeply devoted to the principles of democracy, equality of opportunity in particular, in every aspect of the societal life. In order to achieve this high human quality the person needs a broad education in humanities, non-professional aspects of social sciences as well as natural sciences. A person needs a deep understanding of the purpose of being, truth, honesty, one's place and rights within the society, one's attachment and respect to the nature and environment, and one's unselfishness in social, economic and political spheres of life.

To develop as a democratic person one has to understand, through education, practice, and experience, the complex meaning and application of the principle of equality of opportunity. Because, it is only through the application of this principle that the socio-economic and political framework of each individual's life is determined, expansion of one's freedoms and their limitations are distinguished.

The core part of the education required to understand these values is achieved through an individual's general education extending through the 12th grade. However, in democratic society education is continuous and extends beyond this initial level through all working years of each individual. As part of this continued education, along with technical and professional education, each worker will be required to take each year a certain prescribed number of courses in the areas enhancing his general and cultural knowledge, and updating his knowledge of democracy as applied in daily life.

The other side of a worker's life is related to his work, his professional knowledge, his proficiency, and productiveness. His education in this regard starts when he enters the labor market. There are two aspects to this education. First, a formal technical and professional education which will continue through one's working years until his retirement. For example, if a person wants to become an electrical engineer, he will start his formal higher education as soon as he finishes his 12th grade general education. Each worker starts his professional education full-time when he starts to work and continues thereafter while working. For the first six years he works part-time and after that he works full-time for a period of 30 years, after which he retires from formal employment. However, by no means does this retirement indicate the end of an active and productive life.

During the first six years, after graduation from the 12th grade, the individual continues his education near full-time; let us assume the equivalent of 30 college credits per year, including eight weeks of the summer. Within six years, under the present higher education standards, this amounts to 180 credit hours of education, far beyond what is required now for receiving an engineering or other professional degree. After this period of six years, when the worker assumes a full-time job, he is required to study at least the equivalent of six college credits each semester (two 3-credit courses). One of these two courses relates to his professional area in order to keep him up to date in his field and further expand his technical knowledge, and the other in the liberal arts area, to give him a better understanding of self and society and also to provide him with a better means of enjoyment of life.

This is the course of the individual's formal education which continues at least up to the time of retirement. It is considered as part of his weekly work load.

The other aspect of a worker's education is through experience. Experience at his work place teaches him how he can turn his scientific, cultural, and professional knowledge into efficient and productive action. Experience with the institutions of society outside of his work teaches him how to use his knowledge in the social and natural sciences and humanities for better serving his fellow citizens and his society as a whole, and protect the environment.

Salary Range and Compensation

The minimum salary for a full-time job is based on the amount necessary not only to accommodate the basic needs such as food, housing, clothing, transportation and recreation, but to provide for comfortable living conditions. As stated before, based on the present standards, we may assume an income of $14,000 per person ($7.50 per hour) for this minimum pay. It is obvious that jobs requiring a higher and more specialized education, or harder physical work, would pay a higher salary. As the years of experience and further education is added to the worker's initial level of competence for a full-time job, his salary increases accordingly. But at no time does a worker's pay exceed three times the minimum wage.

Let us assume, for example, that the minimum wage for full-time employment is $15,000; the highest salary would be around $45,000. This means an average salary increase of about 3.4 percent per year. The percent increase in salary will be higher during the early years of work tending toward zero by the end of the 30th year. This will cause younger workers to move faster toward a more convenient life. If we consider economic conditions as those of the United States at present, an annual income of $15,000 will be sufficient to provide an individual with a comfortable living condition as far as the basic needs are concerned. Consider that there is no individual taxation under democratic economy and no property tax to cover the cost of institutions. Thus a $15,000 income is equivalent to about $20,000 under the present federal, state, and local tax systems. One must also consider that there is no social security deductions and no expenditures for the worker's health care, his education and that of his children. Furthermore, each worker receives the equivalent of about $4,000 per year in company shares, from which he also receives benefits. On the other hand, a worker in his mid-career receives an income about $35,000 which would be sufficient to provide for a comfortable life with much higher standards. Here again, since the worker does not pay taxes and receives free health care and education for himself and his children, his $35,000 salary plus returns from his accumulated capital compared to the present standards in the United States, would be equivalent to nearly $50,000.

It is obvious that while nearly all workers start their full-time employment at the level of $15,000 there may be some with higher levels of opportunity which will enter the market at the level of their opportunity based on the extent of education and experience of each. These are usually entering the society from outside. Since through required continuing education and increased experience, the level of competence of a worker continually goes up, so does his level of opportunity and income. The extent of increase in competence determines the amount of increase in salary one receives. This principle applies to all levels of competency. Technical and professional learning can never stop, because in technological society one becomes easily obsolete without updating his knowledge. Remaining at the same level of knowledge is equivalent to decaying in competence. Such behavior will cause lowering of one's level of opportunity and thus the level of his income. This is why continuing education is necessary and required under the democratic economy. Technological society cannot progress or even sustain itself without properly educated and conscious citizens.

CHAPTER 10

FROM SADDAM TO DEMOCRACY

As the years since the Operation Desert Storm have shown, none of the present pressures, whether through economic embargo or military actions, has caused any undermining or actual weakening of Saddam Hastens regime. It is unlikely that the next few years will be any different. There is only one sure way of getting rid of his regime and that is through chipping away his political and military authority and gradually undetermining his power and credibility.

The Iranian Revolution and the Islamic Renaissance

Before discussing as to how to go about dismantling the power structure of Iraq, certain important points affecting the present conditions in the region must be clarified. The first of these is the question of Islamic fundamentalism. The recent surge in Islamic fundamentalism has been a source of worry and discomfort not only to the Western powers but to nearly all the regimes in the area. This has been particularly true in the case of the countries which have vital interests in the region and whose technological development and daily life heavily depend on the availability of energy derived from petroleum. These oil resources are controlled in the Middle East by

Saudi Arabia, Iran, Iraq, Kuwait, and the United Arab Emirates. Saudi Arabia has the largest petroleum reserves and Iran, being second in oil reserves, has a population of about 60 million, much larger than all the others combined. Iran is also the most strategically located country, having an extended border with the countries of the ex-Soviet Union in the north with Iraq and Turkey in the west, and control over all northern shores of the Persian Gulf and the Gulf of Oman. For the latter reason, Iran considers itself the legitimate authority as the guardian of the Persian Gulf and views the presence of foreign powers as an infringement on this legitimate right. Iran believes that the Persian Gulf should be governed by the countries bordering it, the major authority being vested on Iran. Iran has been in the process of developing political and ideological influences among the Central Asian Muslim countries with vast resources and with over 60 million population. Iran has also developed close relations with the state of Azerbaijan with its own oil resources.

This unique strategic position of Iran has always attracted the attention of great Western powers such as Great Britain, France, and Germany; the old Russia and then the Soviet Union, and during the last four decades that of the United States. Presently, both Russia and China have established friendly relations with Iran. France, England, and Germany are trying to recover their prorevolutionary positions, though not their influence. The point is that there cannot be any plan to stabilize the region by leaving out Iran. This country has been and is the pillar of the Middle East diplomacy. It is a country that has kept its independence for nearly 3,000 years and by its high cultural and intellectual heritage has been able to assimilate temporary conquerors in its culture and change them. It has been resentful to outside influence. Two recent examples being the nationalization of oil industries and ousting of the British in the late 1940s and the Americans, who came to the position of influence in 1953 by ousting the democratic government of Dr. Mussaddegh, by the 1979 Islamic Revolution. The point is that in any Middle East policy the position of Iran must be given central and prime consideration. Presently, Iran is governed by the Islamic theologians who place importance on the teachings of the religion. Islam is rich in this regard since Islamic religion is not only a set of religious principles but it is a way of life encompassing from individual self development and purification to societal interactions extending to the process of government. Islam in essence is a system of democratic socialism in which there is no religious hierarchy like those of Christianity. The religion is based on the individual's self and the Creator where human beings have important value yet are a part from the community and responsible for its well being. Any form of government that fits these characteristics of Islam is welcome by the Muslim society where individuals find the government and its policies in harmony with their own religious directions and beliefs and feel at home and comfortable. This has been the secret of endurance of the Islamic government in Iran. In recent Iranian parliamentary elections, held in 1992, some 82 percent of voters participated in the electoral process. A great majority supported governmental policies while ousting nearly one-third of the incumbents. This support comes mainly from the farmers, lower and middle class which altogether form some 85 percent of the population. For the first time in 2,500 years of Iranian history, the rulers do not live in castles with luxury and privileges, they live like a middle class family. There is no apparent corruption among the leaders contrary to those under the previous regime of Mohammed Reza Shah. A regime guided by Islamic fundamentalism is also strongly against any foreign influence in the internal affairs of the country. This policy is very strongly supported by the overwhelming majority of the population. These are all elements that make the Islamic fundamentalism very attractive to ordinary citizens. Iran and Algeria are two outstanding examples.

Islamic fundamentalism is not a new movement. Its last cycle has been since World War I with repeated suppression by the regimes influenced or controlled by the Western powers. The Iranian Revolution of 1979 was the first full success of Islamic fundamentalism in this century. Its development was hampered and badly damaged by the invasion of Iran by Iraq and ensuing costly years of war from 1981 to 1988. Not only the regime did survive but has been trying hard to restructure a wastly destroyed and damaged society. Today it is a well established system and broadly supported by the people.

The Iranian Revolution and the establishment of an Islamic republic has caused an Islamic Renaissance all over the world from Philippine Islands, Indonesia to the whole Middle East and Africa. It has resulted in a surge of activities in Saudi Arabia, Egypt, Sudan, Tunisia, and the Central Asian countries. The fundamentalists succeeded in democratic elections in Algeria then outlawed and deprived from taking over the government.

The point is that the Islamic world will not be the same and will increasingly resent to be influenced or controlled by the Western powers, the United States in particular. The United States as a result of its mistaken polices, is considered the worse enemy of Islam by the people, if not by the government, in many Islamic nations. The present negative attitudes by the government and media does not help the U.S. interests. In any foreign policy decision relating to the Islamic world this fact should be taken into consideration.

The other important point is that not any Islamic fundamentalist regime that may succeed in establishing itself will be under the influence of Iran or even be friendly with Iran. The recent history of Islamic movements illustrates this fact. Each country's interest determines its direction. To think otherwise is like to believe that all Western representative democracies will follow a single policy set by one such as the United States. While all are representative democracies each follows a distinct road prescribed by its national interest and distinct from those of others. As a representative democracy, the Islamic fundamentalist regimes will not be the same but different. For this reason, it is a mistake to think that if Iraq is ruled by the Iraqi Shias, it will fall under the influence of Iran. Those who are knowledgeable about the history and cultures of the area will agree that the Iraqi shias are Arab, quite devoted to the independence of their country despite the fact that they have been suppressed and harshly treated by their own government. However if such a government is formed, it is likely that it will tend to establish friendly relations with Iran, Syria, and Turkey. Nothing better than this could happen for the stability of the Middle East.

Regional Power Structure and the Question of Stability

The third point is the unduly baseless concern about Iran's modernization of its military forces. Iran had a devastating experience with the invasion by Iraq and ensuing war which made Iran conscious of its military weaknesses. The present modernization and expansion of military forces by Iran, considering its size, long borders with different countries, extended seashores, and its large population, is quite nominal compared to the military build-up in Kuwait and Saudi Arabia.

Any thought that Iran may invade its neighbors is groundless. Iran has a much more effective force than the military. It is the success story of the ideology of Islamic Renaissance. Presently, Iran does not have to even attempt to export it to other societies. Many groups in many countries taking Iran as an example of an Islamic republic, are proceeding on their own. If they seek guidance, Iran then responds to it. The Islamic Renaissance has taken root and will continue to grow. A wise American foreign policy has to try to accommodate this fact rather than to oppose it. In regard to Iran, the United States needs to remember the mistake they made in 1953 by overthrowing Dr. Mussaddegh's democratic pro-western government and returning Mohammad Reza Shah to the throne. It deprived Iran from continuation of its newly established democracy and 25 years of harsh dictatorship led to the Revolution of 1979 which caused total exclusion of the United States from the Iranian scene and a deep hatred toward its government.

Islamic Renaissance is expanding rapidly among the Muslim societies and this time it does not seem possible for the Western powers to suppress it. It is a growing political phenomenon deeply attached to socio-cultural values of Islam that the West has to cope with. Countries like Germany, France and Russia with long experience in the region have already understood the importance of this movement and have been forerunners in establishing good relations with Iran. To this list one may add also China, and among Muslim societies, Sudan, Algeria, Syria, Lybia, Azerbaijan, and nearly all the Central Asian countries.

The point in emphasizing the strategic position of Iran and increasing influence of Islamic Renaissance is that in considering the future system of Iraq one must consider this as a positive element. Even with Shias in power, it is very unlikely that Iraq will fall under the influence of Iran. Iraqi Shias are a quite different breed than those of Iran. However, under Shi'it government, Iraq more likely will tend to have close friendly relations with Iran. This is essential to the stability in the region. Iran, Iraq, and Syria will form the pillars of the regional stability. The vital importance of this becomes further clear when one perceives the future instability in Saudi Arabia, Kuwait, and Egypt. The developing trends of Islamic Renaissance in these countries clearly points out to unavoidable future political turmoil and transformation. If the West goes along with the realization of these transformations it may assure a friendly position for itself among these countries. If it opposes, it may retard but not stop the transformation and may end up losing its influence in the area.

From a global policy-making standpoint it is a serious mistake to underestimate the importance and effect of the Islamic Renaissance. According to statistics, Islam is the most rapidly growing religion in the world. For every one person being converted to Christianity, seven are converted into Islam. Being a socialistic, equalitarian and democratic religion, Islam has become highly attractive to depressed, suppressed, deprived, and poor, which comprises nearly 80 percent of the world population. The Islamic Revolution in Iran and the respectable status attained by its government in Iran has awakened these masses about the possibility of what was once considered impossible, namely getting rid of the Western influence and saving the purity of Islamic and the simple life it prescribes, from the contamination brought on it by the imposition of the Western incompatible values. The Islamic revitalization is in process now with a dynamic force behind it, namely the consciousness about its essence and hope for its success in bringing back the Muslim societies to its true adherence and cleaning it from not all but degrading and degenerating norms of the Western cultures. The Islamic Renaissance is in the process of affecting the societies such as Saudi Arabia and Kuwait which live under the primitive tribal interpretation of an advanced religion which created a great civilization with the most scientific and artistic achievement for seven centuries, stretched from Spain, North Africa, the whole Middle East to the heart of India. The present consciousness is mainly based on this historical achievement induced and enlightened by the success of the Islamic Revolution in Iran. Islam, based on its religious principles and evidenced by its historical achievements in its early periods, encouraged scientific inventions and innovations in social, economic, political aspects of the societal life. Islam is also an internationalist religion based on equality of societies and brotherhood.

The point to be stressed by all these is that the Western powers must take Islam, its influence, and its rapid development seriously and consider them important components in the policy-making process if the purpose is to create a stable, harmonious, and peaceful world. Now it is a perfect time for the Western powers to reevaluate their national interests along with their long range objectives.

One strong step toward this aim for the Western countries is to reevaluate such national interests in the Middle East and help, rather than hinder, the establishment of a stable region where the countries of the area can live with one another in peace and friendly relations and could establish sincere relationships with the West on the basis of equality without being subject to exploitation or interference in the internal affairs unless such affairs are determined by the United Nations to be utterly in disregard of human rights and human lives. Such interference should not be induced by one nation like the United States but it has to be by concerted efforts of the Security Council members based on extensive facts and figures and with the support of world opinion expressed by the opinion polls as well as the majority of the nations in the UN General Assembly. Of course, one factor against the realization of a peaceful environment in the Middle East is the loss of many billions of dollars in business of arms sales. This fact might be important for the United States since it is anxious to reduce its high international trade deficit, and creating and sustaining conflicts in the region will boost arm sales.

In light of these presentations, the stability in the Middle East must necessarily include a coalition between Iran, Iraq, and Syria. Iran and Syria already have friendly relations that can be further improved and Iraq is missing from this triangle. To bring Iraq into this triangle several points need to be considered. First, Iran has no territorial claims in Iraq. The treaty of 1975 resolved certain border disputes, especially the sharing of the Shat-al-Arab. This treaty was unilaterally invalidated by Suddam Hussein in 1980 when Iraq invaded Iran, but later just before the Desert Storm Operation, Saddam Hussein revalidated the treaty which is presently in force between the two countries. Second, Iran is not in favor of dividing Iraq into different sectors similar or different from the present division created by the UN by separating Kurds in the north living above the 36th parallel and Shias in the south living below the 32nd parallel line from the central part of the country. Iran has officially objected to such parceling of Iraq and has emphasized its support for the unity of the whole nation despite its ethnic and religious diversities and conflicts.

Third, Syria and Iraq cannot live in peace as long as the Baath Party holds power in Iraq. The reason for such animosity has been discussed before. Finally, and perhaps most importantly, the people of Iraq cannot continue to be subject to extreme and brutal suppression for the sake of realizing the Baath Socialism. The situation is similar, if not harsher than the faith of the Russian people under Stalin. The sufferings have been and continue to be extreme and should not be allowed. The modern world situation is quite different from the past. The advanced information-communication system has joined the world societies together. It has also facilitated the wrongdoings of the governments to be discovered and to be exposed to the world. In modern technological society, human rights have transcended the national borders and has become global, allowing the world community to interfere wherever such rights are harshly and unduly suppressed and abused. The electronic information-communication systems have caused global consciousness about human rights and democratic norms and processes. Thus, they have established a framework for the operation of societies as far as human rights are concerned. One of the most essential of these is the right of the people for self-determination. This right is exercised when people are able to determine their own destiny and their own form of government. Once this right is taken away by a leader or a small group and the society as a whole is suppressed, it is the responsibility and duty of every democratic society to see, through the instrument of the United Nations, that the system is changed and the power is returned to the people. What is going on in Iraq today justifies such action. It is a mistake to assume that if Saddam Hussein is removed things will be better. The problem in Iraq is not Saddam Hussein, it is the Baath Party under which Saddam Hussein has been chosen the sole ruler. Based on the facts presented in this study about the power base of the Baath Party, if he is gone, someone else will be chosen, not by the people, but by the Revolutionary Command Council to take his place as the sole ruler with the same powers working toward the same objectives. As it has been shown, the Interim Constitution was written by the Baath Party to guarantee its sole power to rule the country. There is no single indication that the Party has any intention of giving up power or allowing others to share the power. The history of the last three decades is a living example during which the Baath Party systematically and brutally eliminated all opposition parties and groups and cut off their effective participation in the government.

Toward Democracy in Iraq

The only way to bring democracy to Iraq is to eliminate the dominating power of the Baath Party including that of its designated ruler Saddam Hussein. In this study, a carefully devised form of political system has been proposed with taking into consideration all major religious, ethnic, and economic diversity. It is thought to be the most appropriate form of political system to accommodate diversities while encouraging a democratic process by opening ground and opportunity for it.

The present situation in Iraq offers a unique opportunity to establish the foundation of this government and democratic process. The following is one practical approach but not the only one.

Step 1. Presently, Iraq is divided into three zones by the 32nd and 36th parallels. Even though the 36th parallel was established as a dividing line to provide a sector of territory where Kurds could live and function with some protection from Saddam Hussein's suppression, most of the Kurds still live below this parallel line in the governorates of Sulaymaniyah, Tameeem, Salah al Deer, and Dialur. Presently, only the two Kurdish governorates of D'Hok and Arbil are above the 36th parallel line. Therefore, a large number of Kurds are still under suppression of Saddam Hussein. In order to protect most of the Kurds it would be justifiable to move the dividing line from the 36th to the 35th parallel. This will locate nearly 80 percent of the Kurds above the line. It is not difficult for the Security Council to change this line since atrocities committed by Saddam against the Kurds below the 36th parallel is numerous and continuous. Another very important consequence of this change is that it will take the oil fields of the north out of Saddam's authority. This will cause great economic problems for Saddam since he will be totally deprived of the revenues from oil. On the other hand, the revenues from oil will boost the economies of the north and south accelerating the downfall of Saddam and the Baath Party.

Step 2. To allow the people in the north and the south opportunity to express their opinions. To achieve this aim, the UN Security Council must try to reduce Saddam's ruling power in these areas by gradually imposing limitations on the operation of and suppression by the Iraqi military. This could start by prohibiting the movement of military units and equipment from the central part to these areas and imposing limitations on the size of the military unit that could be located in these areas. These steps all can be legally taken under the cease fire agreement with Iraq according to which Iraq is prohibited to suppress the Kurds in the north and Shias in the south.

Step 3. Considering the federal system proposed in this study, the UN Security Council to call directly or to induce indirectly the peoples above the 35th parallel and below the 32nd parallel to send delegates to Amadiya or any other secure place in the north or the south to form a Constituent Assembly for formulating and adapting a constitution and taking steps toward formation of a new federal system, the United Republics of Iraq. The size of membership in the Constituent Assembly will be based on the population of each district within the federal territory of the government to be constituted as presented in Figure 10-1. Table 10-1 presents these allocations.

As illustrated in Table 10-1 the population below the 32nd parallel and above the 35th parallel consist of about 52 percent of the total population of Iraq thus forming the majority of population. Representatives in the National Constituent Assembly also is 84 seats out of a total of 163 seats figured for the National House of Representatives of the new National Government or 52 percent. Thus, the majority of the population represented by the majority of the seats in the future National House of Representatives give legitimacy to decisions of the National Constituent Assembly.

The problem arises when the northern zone is determined by the 36th parallel instead of the 35th. In this case the population of the two zones combined will be 42 percent of the total, the same being the ratio of representatives in the National Constituent Assembly and that of the future National House of Representatives. For this reason alone the moving of the zone from the 36th to the 35th parallel is utmost important.

If the northern territory is extended to the 35th parallel line, four of the six states can be effectively established and made operational by the National Constituent Assembly according to the new constitution. This system will place also all oil resources within the territory and under the authority of the new government and the respective republics.

Under the 35th parallel zone method only the Republic C and District of Baghdad will remain in the hands of the old regime.

Figure 10-1. Territory of Iraq divided by the two northern and southern zones.

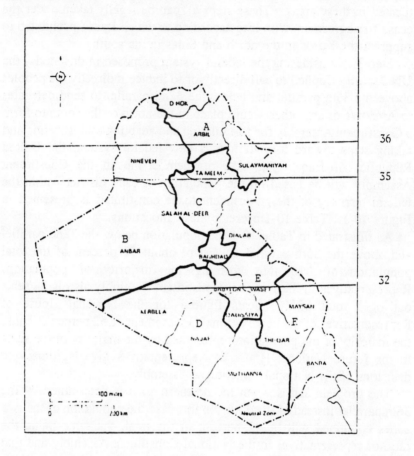

Republic E will be divided between the old and the new regimes. However, provisional government for this territory can be established following the method used by the other new republics. This government will have authority within the territory located to the south of the 32nd parallel comprising about 35 percent of the population of Republic E. (See Figure 10-1.)

Considering the complex ethnic and religious problems and the importance of time, it seems appropriate that the constitutional provisions proposed in this study be adopted as an Interim Constitution

Table 10-1. Memberships in the National Constituent Assembly from Each District

| A. From the Northern Zone | | No. of Representatives | |
District	Population	25th Parallel Zone	36th Parallel Zone
Duhak	293	3	3
Arbil	743	7	7
Sulaymaniya	943	9	-
Temeen	593	6	-
Nineveh	1507	15	15
B. From the Southern Zone			
Kerbela	456	5	5
Najaf	723	7	7
Muthanna	313	3	3
Qadissiya	561	6	6
Maysan	500	5	5
Dhi Qar	918	9	9
Basra	872	9	9
Total	8422	84	69
Percent of total Iraqi Population	52	52	42

Source: From tables 5-2 and 6-1

Table 10-2. Percent of Population of Each Republic Controlled by its New Government

| Republics | Percent of Population of each Republic | |
	35th parallel zone	36th parallel zone
A	90	75
B	65	34
C	27	0
D	90	90
E	34	34
F	96	96

Source: Calculated by using Tables 5-2, 6-1, and 9-1.

subject to revision later on. The Constituent Assembly will then elect an Acting President for the nation and will constitute itself as an Interim National Assembly. The country will be named the United

Republics of Iraq. The president will represent the whole nation. The Assembly will represent the participating states and new representatives will be added to it as the other states join the federation. State A and a good part from State B are above the 35th parallel, States D and E are nearly all below the 32nd parallel. This constitutes four out of the six states forming the federation.

According to Table 10-1, state A will have 19 representatives, State B will have 15 counting only the district of Nineveh which is located to the north of the 35th parallel. State D will have 15 and State F, 23 representatives. These all together still constitute a National Assembly of 72 representatives. The District of Tameen from State C is located above the 35th parallel. It may volunteer to represent State C. In this case it will have six representatives from a total of 22 allocated to State C. In the same manner District of Qadissiya from State E may volunteer to represent this state. In this case it will have six representatives out of 22 allocated to State E. By this way, all the states will be represented in the National Assembly. The number of representatives will increase as the rest of the territories join the federation. The representatives will be elected by the manner prescribed in Chapter Six.

Concerning the obstacles for the first popular election of the President of the United Republics, it seems appropriate that the first president be chosen by the first National Assembly. Once state governments are established and electoral laws are enacted then the presidential election will be subject to popular vote as proposed in Chapter Seven or as the National Assembly may prescribe. No outside opposition group which is not presently active within the territory will be allowed to participate in the electoral process. However, any member of the opposition group who is a resident in Iraq may present himself as a candidate from his district of residence.

More than half of the population of the country live within these territories and based on the above calculations they occupy 85 seats out of the total number of 163 seats for the whole country. The representatives will be elected through the method of proportional representation from each electoral district as follows and as prescribed in Chapter Six.

The Constituent Assembly will create an executive Council which will make rules and regulations and supervise the first National

Table 10-3. Number of Electoral Districs in each Territorial District within Each Republic

		No. of Seats	No. of Districts	No from each District
A	Dabuk	3	1	3
	Arbil	7	2	3 & 4
	Sulaymaniyah	9	3	3 each
	At large	1	-	-
B	Ninevah	15	5	3 each
C	Tameem	6	2	3 each
D	Karbala	5	1	5
	Najaf	7	2	3 & 4
	Muthanna	3	1	3
E	Qadissiya	6	2	3 each
F	Maysan	5	1	5
		9	3	3 each
		9	3	3 each
Total Seats		85	26	85

Assembly elections. The Council will consist of two members from each of the states of A, D, and F and one member from each of the states of B, C, and E a total of nine members. The Council will elect a President from among its members. The First National Assembly will convene immediately after the elections and will choose an Interim President for the United Republics of Iraq. The national government then will start operation as prescribed by the Constitution. It will take authority over the production and marketing of the petroleum, the revenues of which will be distributed and spent as prescribed by the constitution.

Each state will follow the same procedures. It will form a state Constituent Assembly with delegates from each district. It will write the State Constitution and then will choose an Executive Council to supervise the first Assembly elections. The first State Assembly will select an Interim Governor which will act as the state Chief Executive until a governor is elected by popular vote as prescribed by the State Constitution. In each state the government will take over the national bureaucracies of the old regime and transform them to state administrative systems as it sees fit. the military forces of the old regime may be given the opportunity to join the new national government. The prospect of economic prosperity of the new states may be an important inducement for such action. Until the state governments are well established and capable of assuming the responsibility of self-government, the new national government will rule while providing means and facilitating the process of self-government for the states.

The formation of the United Republics of Iraq will have several effects upon the rest of the territory. First, it will represent the majority of the population of the country, therefore, being a legitimate form of government. Second, it will go out of the sphere of economic embargo and will start rapid development in every aspect of life by using its oil resources and establishing commercial relations with other countries. Third, by the betterment of living conditions within its territories and the enjoyment of political, economic, and social freedom by its citizens, it will induce the rest of the country to Join it. Fourth, deprived from its oil resources and its access to the outside world, the power of Saddam and the Baath Party will be undermined and more likely his military forces will rise against him or join the new government. In either case the old government will be toppled. Fifth, the new government will start to establish its own military forces which may cause, very likely, Saddam's forces to join them.

Ultimately, in a short time, more likely within two to three years, the whole country will become united under one flag with the best model of democracy in the region. This form of democratic federalism will affect the neighboring countries, especially those in the south forcing them to modify their form of government in order to satisfy the aspirations of their people.

From a regional security viewpoint, peace and friendship between Iraq and Iran will establish the base of the regional power in the area, will bring democracy to other countries in the region and guarantee peace and stability. It is more likely that after the fall of the Baath Party in Iraq, Syria will join Iraq and Iran and a triangle of diplomatic power will be established.

Some Western countries including the United States may not like this development even though it guarantees peace and stability in the region. By the fall of dictatorial regimes in Kuwait, Saudi Arabia, and Egypt, the United States will lose its influence in the region. The Persian Gulf will come under the guardianship of Iran since it controls most of its shores and historically it dominated the Gulf, before the Revolution, under Mohammed Reza Shah. However, if the United

States in its policy-making process avoids to interfere in domestic and regional politics and treats other countries on the basis of equality, it may not be difficult for it to establish friendly relationships with the countries of the Middle East especially with Iran and Iraq. An essential step toward this purpose would be the solution of the Arab-Israeli conflict by providing a homeland for the Palestinians and playing an impartial role in resolving the conflict. Afterward, the United States must maintain its relations with all the countries of the region on the basis of equality and fairness without allowing a privileged position to Israel. Policies backed by force, whether diplomatic, economic, or military, have made the United States an enemy in the eyes of nearly all Third World countries. The United States may have the government of some of these countries on its side by different kinds of inducements, mostly money, but it has caused an increasing animosity from the part of the people. Included are all Latin American countries, nearly all African countries, all the countries of the Middle East except Israel. It follows the same wrong policy in Russia and Central Asian countries which in the long run will turn the people of these societies against the United States. In this electronic and satellite information-communication era, where the information system has become global, the national and individual consciousness of the old traditional societies have been awakened using a revolution of rising expectations from political, social, and economic viewpoints. From the political standpoint, people are becoming aware of individual rights and democratic values and processes. It is becoming more and more difficult to sustain dictatorship. Global human rights organizations and policies of the United Nations agencies feed and accelerate this process of democratization. From the social viewpoint the rising expectations have created increasing demands for free and available education, national health care, housing, transportation, employment opportunities, and old age benefits. From the economic standpoint there has developed a keen awareness of the dominance of foreign institutions and a small domestic economic elite over the resources of the country and the need to eradicate poverty and diminish class stratification by liberating national resources. There is a growing anticapitalistic sentiment in the world which does not encompass only the less developed countries but those of Europe and to a much lesser degree the United States. Capitalism is considered the cause of concentration of wealth and power in the hands of a few to the detriment of the rest of the world. It has been looked upon as the main cause of exploitation of the Third World countries by giant economic organizations of the advanced societies particularly those of the United States.

All these phenomenal changes during the last two decades mandate a new and appropriate approach to foreign policy. A good foreign policy is the one that stays one step ahead of changes rather than tracing them. To be able to make such policies, the United State and the West must try to understand the regional societies. This can be done only by knowing the history, culture, language, literature, religion and deep rooted customs of diversified communities. For example, looking at the historical background and geographical situation and the rules of international law it is quite logical for Iran to claim hegemony in the Persian Gulf. On the same ground it seems quite illogical for the United States or any other Western country to take over the guardianship of the Gulf. How would the United states feel if the Gulf of Mexico was dominated by Iran, Russia or any other country? Hegemony over the Persian Gulf does not give Iran an absolute power over the operation of the Gulf but recognize Iran as an authority to enforce international laws and regulations in relation to freedom of navigation, regulation of fishing and other aspects of operation in the Gulf. International laws of the seas recognized the right of each country to its shores in the Persian Gulf. If the Persian Gulf needs a collective force to supervise it and enforce the laws it should be a collective force from the countries of the Gulf in which Iran would have the majority voice because it has authority over the most of the shores in the Gulf. All other countries should keep their forces outside of the Persian Gulf. The United Nations should be the sole authority to resolve the conflicts among the Gulf countries with the last option to resort to force. The modern technological age, with a global consciousness does not allow or justify one country, regardless how powerful, to lead the world. It is increasingly and rapidly becoming a world of the united nations with consensus, reason, and wisdom as the bases for international relations rather than the use of force whether economic, diplomatic, or military. On this basis the concept of self determination of the nations is receiving a new interpretation. If the government of a nation is not established by the consent of its people and human rights are not respected and protected by such government, the world community feels responsible in providing means to return that government of its people. Iraq fits this situation. The same responsibility applies when a nation is suppressed or overrun by another or an ethnic group is involved in inhuman acts against the life, liberty , and property of innocent people. Bosnia Herzegovina provides an example.

Footnotes

Preface

[1]The following publications are credited for most of the information about Iran. Federal Research Division, Library of Congress, Helen Chapin Metz, ed., *Iran: A Country Study*, Washington, D.C.: Govenment Printing Office, 1989; for details see pp. 195-234. Cyrus Bina and Hamid Zangeneh, *Modern Capitalism and Islamic Ideology in Iran*, New York: St. Martin's Press, 1992; for details see pp. 22-43.

Chapter One

[1]For those not familiar with the geography of the time, the present name of the territories are given for easy recognition.

Chapter Four

[1]Rezazadeh, *Technological Democracy*, pp. 217-257.
[2]T.H. Marshall, p. 72
[3]Agbese, p. 41.

[4]Amin, 1974 & 76; Baran; Delacroix and Ragin; Evans and Timberlake.

[5]Lipset, 1967; Rezazadeh, *Technodemocratic Econimic Theory*, pp. 180-190.

[6]Linz, *Breakdown of Democratic Regimes*, p. 16.

[7]Ibid, p. 20.

[8]Lipset, *Politician Man*, pp. 68-71.

[9]Dahl, *Polyarchy*, pp. 129-150.

[10]Jonathan Hartlyn, "Colombia: The Politics of Violence and Accomodation," in Diamond, Linz, and Lipset, *Democracy in Developing Countries: Latin America*, pp. 310-311. Reza Rezazadeh, "Local Administration in Colombia," *Journal of Administratoin Overseas*, April 1970, Vol. IX, No. 2, p. 110.

[11]Larry Diamond, Juan J. Linz, Seymour Martin Lipset, *Polictics in Developing Countries: Comparing Experiences with Democracy*, pp. 14-15.

[12]Juan Linz, and Alfred Stepan, eds., *The Breakdown of Democratic Regimes*, 4 vols. (Baltimore, MD: John Hopkins University Press, 1978).

[13]Ibid., pp. 27-38.

[14]John Booth, " Costa Rica: The Roots of Democratic Stability," in Diamond, Linz, and Kipset, *Democracy in Developing Countries: Latin America*, pp. 402-404.

[15]Levine, "Venezuela," pp. 278-279.

[16]Holm, "Botzwana," p. 195.

[17]Lipset, *Politica Man*, p. 45.

[18]Dahl, *Polyarchy*, p. 81.

[19]Samuel P. Huntington, *Political Order in Changing Societies*, (New Haven, CT: Yale University Press, 1968), p. 5.

[20]Michael P. Todaro, *Economic Developemtn in the Third World*, 2nd ed. (New York: Longman, 1981), p. 165.

[21]Levine, "Venezuela," pp. 279-280.

[22]Lipset, *First New Nation*, pp. 307-308.

[23]Linz, *Breakdown of Democratic Regimes*, p. 24; Rezazadeh and J. M. McKenzie, *Political Parties in Colombia*, pp. 1-44, 61, 70-74.

[24]Giovanni Sartori, *Parties and Party Systems: A Framework for Analysis*, (Cambridge: Cambridge University Press, 1976), pp. 131-140.

[25]Powell, *Contemporary Democracies*, pp. 154-157.

[26]Huntington, *Political Order in Changing Societies*, pp. 12-24. See Reza Rezazadeh, *Technological Democracy: A Humanistic Philosophy of the Future Society*, (New York: Vantage Press, 1990), pp. 156-166; Reza Rezazadeh, *Technodemocratic Economic Tehory: From Capitalism and Socialism to Democracy*, (Platteville, WI: Eternalist Foundation, 1991), pp. 297-310.

[27]See, for example, Robert Packenham, *Liberal America and the Third World: Political Development Ideas in Foreign Aid and Social Science*, (Princeton, NJ: Princeton Univeristy Press, 1973).

[28]Dahle, *Polyarchy*, p. 197.

[29]Robert Fatton, Jr., "Bringing the Ruling Class Back In: Class, State, and Hegemony in Africa," *Comparative Policitcs*, 29 (April 1988); pp. 253-264.

[30]Vernon Loeb, "Asian Nations Inventing Their Own Democracy," *Night-Rider Newspapers* in Wisconsin State Journal, June 14, 1992. p. 2-E.

[31]Ibid.

[32]Ibid.

[33]Ibid.

[34]Richard Robinson, "Authoritarian States, Capital-Owning Classes, and the Politics of Newly Industrialized Countries: The Case of Indonesia," *World Politics* 41, 1 (October 1988), pp. 52-74.

[35]Jean Guaryras, "Bidding Farewell to Khomeini's Revolutions," *Manchester Guardian Weekly*, May 3, 1992, p. 13.

[36]Ibid.

[37]Jean Guayras, "Elections Set Seal on Rafsanjani's Victory Against the Radicals," *Manchester Guardian Weekly*, April 26, 1992, p. 13.

[38]Martin Wooliacott, "Iran's Saving Graces are Women Under Wraps," *Manchester Guardian Weekly*, April 26, 1992, p. 8.

[39]For the situation in other Latin American countries see Roberto Fabricio, "Latin America Teeters Between Reform, Polpulism," *Wisconsin State Journal*, May 31, 1992, p. 2-B. See also Frank Tachau, *Turkey: The Politics of Authority, Democracy and Development*, (New Yrok: Praeger, 1984).

Chapter Five

[1]Cahpin Metz, Helen ed. *Iraq: A Country Study*, 4th ed. Federal Research Division, Library of Congress, Washington, D.C.: U.S. Government Printing Office, 1990, pp. 241-256.

[2]Samir al-Khalil, *Republic of Fear: The Politics of Modern Iraq*, Berkeley, Cal.: Univeristy of California Press, 1989, pp. 3-72.

[3]Ibid, p. 20.

[4]The percentage of participation, exceptionally rose to 55 percent in 1992 presidential elections.

[5]*Citizen and Politics: A view From Main Street America*, (The Harwood Group, The Kettering Foundation, 1991).

[6]Ibid.

Chapter Six

[1]*The Iraqi Interm Constitution*, Art. 37.

[2]Ibid, Art. 38.

[3]Ibid, Art. 41.

[4]Ibid.

[5]Ibid, Art. 42.

[6]Ibid, Art. 43.

[7]Ibid, Art. 44.

[8]Ibid, Art. 46.

[9]Ibid, Art. 47.

[10]Ibid, Art. 51.

[11]Ibid, Art. 52.

[12]Ibid, Art. 53.

[13]Ibid, Art. 37.

[14]Ibid, Art. 38.

[15]Ibid, Art. 56.

[16]Ibid, Art. 19(b).

[17]Ibid, Art. 20(a).

[18]Ibid, Art. 20(b).

[19]Ibid, Art. 22(a).

[20]Ibid, Art. 22(b).

[21]Ibid, Art. 22(b).

[22]Ibid, Art. 22(c).

[23]Ibid, Art. 26.

[24]Ibid.

[25]An amended version from the *Constituion of the Islamic Republic of Iran*, Art. 57.

[26]*The Constitution of the Islamic Republic of Iran*, Art. 70.

[27]Ibid, Art. 87 modified.

[28]Ibid, Art. 88 modified.

[29]Ibid, Art. 89 modified.

[30]Ibid, ammended.

[31]*The Constitution of the United States*, Art. I, Sec. 4.

[32]Ibid, Sec. 5.

[33]Ibid.

[34]Ibid.

[35]Ibid, Sec. 6.

[36]Ibid, ammended.

[37]Ibid., Sec. 7 ammended.

[38]Ibid., Sec. 8 ammended.

[39]Ibid, Sec. 9.

[40]Ibid.

[41]*The Constitution of the Islamic Republic of Iran*, Art. 85.

[42]Ibid.

Chapter 7

[1]*The Constituion of the United States*, Art. II, Sec. 1 revised.

[2]Ibid.

[3]Ibid, revised.

[4]*The Constitution of the Islamic Republic of Iran*, Art. 121, revised.

[5]Ibid, Art. 122, revised.

[6]Ibid, Art. 124.

[7]Ibid, Art. 126, revised.

[8]Ibid, Art. 127, revised.

[9]Ibid, Art. 128, revised.

[10]Ibid, Art. 134, revised.

[11]Ibid, Art. 135, revised.

[12]Ibid, Art. 136, revised.

[13]Ibid, Art. 137, revised.

[14]Ibid, Art. 138, revised.

[15]Ibid, Art. 140, revised.

[16]Ibid, Art. 141, revised.
[17]Ibid, Art. 142, revised.
[18]*The Constitution of the United States*, Art. II, Sec. 2, revised.
[19]Ibid, revised.
[20]Ibid, Sec. 3, revised.
[21]Ibid, Art. III, Sec. 1, revised.
[22]Ibid, Sec. 2, revised.
[23]Ibid, revised.
[24]*The Constitution of the Islamic Republic of Iran*, (1988), Art. 162, revised.
[25]Ibid, Art. 164, revised.
[26]Ibid, Art. 173, revised.
[27]*The Constitution of the United States*, The Preamble, revised.
[28]*The Interim Constitution of Iraq*, Art. 1, revised.
[29]Ibid, Art. 2, revised.
[30]Ibid, Art. 4, revised.
[31]Ibid, Art. 5, revised.
[32]Ibid, Art. 7, revised.
[33]Ibid, Art. 9, revised.
[34]*The Constitution of the United States*, Art. I, Sec. 10, revised.
[35]Ibid, revised.
[36]Ibid, revised.

Chapter Eight

[1]Article 1.
[2]This statement is based on the Baath Party's dream of forming an Arab Nation encompassing all Arab countries of which Iraq would be a part.
[3]Article 5.
[4]Ibid.
[5]For details of the theory see Reza Rezazadeh, *Technological Democracy* (1990) and *Technodemocratic Economic Theory* (1991).
[6]*Interim Constitution*, Article 20.
[7]*U.S. Constitution*, 14th Amendment, Sec. 1.
[8]*Iraqi Interim Constitution*, Art. 21(b).
[9]*U.S. Constitution*, 13th Amendment, Sec. 1.
[10]*Iraqi Interim Constitution*, Art. 22(b).

[11]Ibid, Art. 27(a).

[12]Ibid, Art. 27(b).

[13]Ibid, Art. 27(c).

[14]Ibid, Art. 31(a).

[15]Ibid, Art. 31(b).

[16]Thomas R. Dye, *Who's Running America?*, 4th ed., Englewood Cliffs, NJ: Prentice Hall, 1986.

[17]Reza Rezazadeh, *Technological Democracy: A Humanistic Philosophy of the Future Society*, 1990; *Technodemocratic Economic Theory: From Capitalism and Socialism to Democracy*, 1991.

[18]For this educatioal system see Reza Rezazadeh, *Technological Democracy*,pp. 37-38, 293-297, and 31; *Technodemocratic Economic Theory*, pp. 228-231, 270-272.

[19]Ibid, 146-147, 290-293; 272-273, 292.

[20]Reza Rezazadeh, *Technological Democracy*,pp. 194-208.

[21]Reza Rezazadeh, *Technological Democracy*,pp. 192-193; *Technodemocratic Economic Theory*, pp. 231-235, 219.

[22]Reza Rezazadeh, *Technodemocratic Economic Theory*, pp. 78-91.

[23]Ibid, pp. 334-337.

[24]Ibid.

[25]John McDermott, "Technology: The Opiate of the Intellectuals," in Albert H. Teich, ed., 3rd ed., *Technology and Man's Future*, (New York: St. Martin's Press, 1981), pp. 144-148.

Chapter 9

[1]See for example, Michael Parenti, *Democracy for the Few*, 4th ed., New York: St. Martin's Press, 1983, pp. 182-198; and Thomas R. Dye, *Who's Running America?*, 5th ed., Englewood Cliffs, NJ: Prentice-Hall, 1990, pp. 116-137.

[2]For more informaiton see Reza Rezazadeh, *Technodemocratic Economic Theory*, pp. 5-21, 171-179; also Michael Parenti, *Democracy for the Few*, pp. 199-223; and Thomas R. Dye, *Who's Running America*, pp. 222-247.

[3]See Thomas R. Dye, *Who's Running America?*, pp. 15-63; Michael Parenti, *Democracy for the Few*, pp. 9-38.

[4]For details see Reza Rezazadeh, *Technodemocratic Economic Theory*, pp. 183-184 and 199-205.

[5]Ibid, pp. 212-213.

Bibliography

Books

Abdulghani, Jasim M. *Iraq and Iran: The Years of Crisis*. Baltimore: John Hopkins University Press, 1984.

Abu Jaber, Kemal. *The Arab Baath Scoialist Party*. Syracuse University Press, 1966.

Adams, Doris Goodrich. *Iraq's People and Resources*. (Unieristy of California Publications in Economics, XVIII). Berkeley: Univeristy of California Press, 1958.

Adams, Henry. *Democracy*. New York: NAL Penguin, Inc., 1983.

Alnasrawi, Abbas. *Financing Economic Development in Iraq: The Role of Oil in a Middle Eastern Economy*. New York: Praeger, 1967.

Amin, Samir. *Imperialism and Unequal Development*. New York: Monthly Review Press, 1977.

Arendt, Hannah. *The Human Condition*. Chicago: University of Chicago Press, 1970.

Armajani, Yahya, and Thomas M. Ricks. *Middle East: Past and Present*, 2nd Ed. Englewood, New Jersey: Prentice-Hall, 1980.

Atkinson, A.B. *The Economics of Inequality*. New York: Oxford Univeristy Press, 1975.

Axelgard, Frederick W. (ed.) *Iraq in Transition: A Political, Economic and Strategic Perspective*. Boulder, Colorado: Westview Press, 1986.

El-Azhary, M.S. *The Iran-Iraq War: An Historical, Economic, and Political Analysis*. New York: St. Martin's Press, 1984.

Bachrach, Peter. *The Theory of Democratic Elitism*. Boston: Little, Brown, 1967.

Baran, Paul A., and Paul M. Sweezy. *Monopoly Captial: An Essay on the American Economics and Social Order*. New York: Monthly Review Press, 1966.

Batatu, Hanna. *The Old Social Classes and the Revolutionary Movement of Iraq: A Study of Iraq's Old Landed and Commercial Classes and of its Communists, Baathists, and Free Officers*. Princeton: Princeton University Press, 1978.

Bauer, P.T. *Equality, the Third World, and Economic Delusion*. Cambridge, Massachusetts: Harvard Univeristy Press, 1981.

Beaumont, Peter, Gerald H. Blake, and J. Malcolm Wagstaff. *The Middle East: A Geographical Study*, 2nd ed. New York: Halsted Press, 1988.

Bernstein, Eduard. *Evolutionary Socialism*. Translated by E.C. Harvey-B.W. Huebsch, New York: 1909.

Bettelheim, Charles. *Economic Calcuation and Forms of Property: An Essay on the Transition Between Capitalism and Socialism*. New York: Monthly Review Press, 1974.

Bookchin, M. *The Ecology of Freedom*. Palo Alto, California: Chesire Books, 1982.

Braverman, Harry. *Labor and Monopoly Capital: The Degradation of Work in the Twentieth Century*. New York: Monthly Review Press, 1976.

Bretton, H.L. *The Power of Money*. New York: State University of New York Press, 1980.

Buchanan, James M. *Democracy in Deficit*. San Diego, California: Academic Press, 1977.

Caraellil, M. Dino and John G. Morris (eds.), European Colloquy for

Direcotrs of National Research Institute in Education. *Equality of Opporutnity Reconsidered: Values in Education for Tomarrow*. Netherlands: Swets and Zeitinger, 1979.

Carnoy, Martin, and Derek Sheafer. *Economic Democracy: The Challenge of the 1980s*. White Plains, New York: Middle East Sharpe, 1980.

Chapin Metz, Helen, ed. *Iraq: A Country Study*, 4th ed. Federal Research Division, Library of Congress. Washington, D.C.: U.S. Government Printing Office, 1990.

Clecak, Peter. *Crooked Paths: Reflections on Socialism, Conservatism, and the Welfare State*. New York: Hraper and Row, 1977.

Cnudde, Charles F. and Deane E. Neubauer. *Empirical Democratic Theory*. Chicago: Markham, 1969.

Cohen, Carl. *Communism, Fascism, and Democracy*. 2nd ed. New York: Random House 1972.

Cohen, Marshall. *Equality and Preferential Treatment*. Princeton, New Jersey: Princeton University Press, 1976.

Coleman, James S. *Equality of Educational Opportunity*. Totowa, New Jersey: Littlefield, 1973.

Commoner, Barry. *Poverty of Power*. New York: Knopf, 1976.

Conley, Patrick T. *Democracy in Decline*. Providence: Rhode Island Publications in Society, 1977.

Cordesman, Anthony H. *The Iran-Iraq War: 1984-1986*. Rosslyn, Virginia: Baton Analytical Assessments Center, 1986.

Coulter, P. *Social Mobilization and Liberal Democracy*. Lexington: Lexington Books, 1975.

Dann, Uriel. *Iraq Under Qassem, 1958-63*. New Yrok: Praeger, 1969.

Denitch, Bodgan, ed. *Democratic Socialism: The Mass Left in Advanced Industrial Societies*. Allanheld: Osmun and Company, 1981.

Devlin, John. *The Baath Party: A History from Its Origins to 1966*. Stanford: Hoover Institution Press, 1976.

Doel, Hans Van Den. *Democracy and Welfare Economics*. Cambridge, Massachusetts: Cambridge University Press, 1979.

Drucker, P.F., and others. *Power and Democracy in America*.

Westport, Connecticut: Greenwood Press, 1976.

Drysdale, Adlasdair and Gerald H. Blake. *The Middle East and North Africa: A Political Geography*. London: Oxford University Press, 1985.

Dumbauld, Edward, ed. *The Political Writings of Thomas Jefferson*. New York: Liberal Arts Press, 1956.

Durbin, E.F.M. *The Politics of Democratic Socialism*. London: Routledge and Kegan Paul, 1940.

Dye, Thomas R. *Who's Running America? The Conservative Years*. 4th ed. Englewood Cliffs, New Jersey: Prentice-Hall, 1986.

Economist Intelligence Unit. *Iraq: Contry Report, 1988*. No. 1, London: 1988.

Encel, Solomon. *Equality and Authority*. London, Tavistock, Publications, 1970.

Feinberg, Walter. *Equality and Social Policy*. Champaign: Univeristy of Illinois Press, 1978.

Fields, G.S. *Poverty, Inequality, and Development*. Cambridge, Massachusetts: Cambridge University Press, 1980.

Freedman, Robert. *The Marxist System: Economic, Political, and Social Perspectives*. Chatham, New Jersey: Chatham House Publishers, 1990.

Gabbey, Rony. *Communism and Agrarian Reform in Iraq*. London: Croom Helm, 1978.

Gallman, Waldemar. *Iraq Under General Nuri*. Baltimore: Johns Hopkins University Press, 1964.

Garvin, A.P. *How to Win with Information or Lose Without It*. Washington, D.C.: Bermont Books, 1980.

Ghareeb, Edmond, ed. *Split Vision: Arab Portrayal in the American Media*. Washington, D.C.: The Institute of Middle Eastern and African Affairs, 1977.

_____. *The Kurdish Question in Iraq*. Syracuse: Syracuse University Press, 1981.

Graham, Otis L. *Towrd a Planned Society: From Roosevelt to Nixon*. New York. Oxford Univeristy Press, 1977.

Haddad, George M. *Revolution and Military Rule in the Middle East*, Vol. II: The Arab States. New York: Robert Speller & Sons, 1971.

Haksar, Vinit. *Equality, Liberty and Perfectionism*. Oxford: Oxford

University Press, 1979.

Hale, Matthew, Dr. *Human Science and Social Order*. Philadelphia, Pennsylvania: Temple University Press, 1980.

Harrington, Michael. *Socialism*. New York: Dutton, 1972.

_____. *The Twilight of Capitalism*. New Yrok: Simon and Schuster, 1977.

Hayek, Freidrich A. *Constitution of Liberty*. Chicago: University of Chicago Press, 1960.

_____. *Road to Serfdom*. Chicago: University of Chicago Press, 1949.

_____. *Social Justice Socialism and Democracy*. Terramurse, Australia: Center of Independent Studies, 1979.

Helms, Christine Moss. *Iraq, Eastern Flank of the Arab World*. Washington: Brookings Institution, 1984.

Hitti, Philip K. *The Near East in History*. New Jersey: Van Jostrand, 1961.

Hughes, John F. *Equal Edcucation*. Bloomington: Indiana Universtiy Press, 1973.

Hurst, Charles E. *The Anatomy of Social Inequality*. St. Louis: Mosby, 1979.

International Institute for Strategic Studies. *The Military Balance, 1979-1980*. London: 1979.

_____. *The Military Balance, 1985-1986*. London: 1985.

_____. Ministry of Planning. Central Statistical Organization. *Annual Abstract of Statistics, 1985*. Baghdad: n.d.

Ireland, Philip. *Iraq: A Study in Political Development*. New York: Macmillan, 1938.

Ismael, Tareq Y. *Iraq and Iran: Roots of Conflict*. Syracuse: Syracuse University Press, 1982.

Jackson, Robert W. *Political and Social Equality: A Comparative Analysis*. New York: Wiley, 1975.

Jawad, Saad. *Iraq and the Kurdish Question, 1958-1970*. London: Ithaca Press, 1981.

Joseph, Keith and Jonathan Sumpton. *Equality*. London: John Murray, 1979.

Judson, H.F. *The Search for Solutions*. New York: Holt, Rinehart and Winston, 1980.

Kanowitz, Leo. *Equal Rights: The Male Stake*. Albuquerque:

University of New Mexico Press, 1981.

Kariel, Henry. *The Decline of American Pluralism*. Stanford, California: Stanford University Press, 1961.

Kelidar, Abbas. *The Integration of Modern Iraq*. New York: St. Martin's Press, 1979.

Khadduri, Majid. *Repulican Iraq*. London: Oxford University Press, 1969.

_____. *Socialist Iraq: A Study in Iraqi Politics Since 1968*. Washington: Middle East Institute, 1978.

Kolki, Gabriel. *Wealth and Power in America*. New York: Praeger, 1962.

Kozol, Jonathan. *Illiterate America*. Garden City, New York: Anchor Press/Doubleday, 1985.

Lecky, William E.H. *Democracy and Liberty*. Indianapolis, Indiana: Liberty Fund 1896. Reprint, 1981.

Leiss, William. *The Domination of Nature*. New York: Braziller, George, Inc., 1972.

_____. *The Limits of Satisfaction*. Toronto: Univeristy of Toronto Press, 1976.

Lindsay, A.D. *The Essentials of Democracy*. Oxford: Claredon Press, 1929.

Lovings, Amory. *Soft Energy Paths: Toward a Durable Peace*. Cambridge, Massachusetts: Ballinger Publications, 1977.

Machlup, Fritz. *The Produciton and Distribution of Knowldge*. Princeton, New Jersey: PRinceton University Press, 1962.

Marcuse, Hubert. *One Dimensional Man*. Boston: Beacon Press, 1964.

Marr, Phebe. *The Modern History of Iraq*. Boulder, Colorado: Westview Press, 1985.

Mayo, Henry B. *An Introduction to Democratic Theory*. New York: Oxford Univeristy Press, 1960.

McDonald, J. Ramsay. *Parliament and Democracy*. Manchester, England: National Labour Press, 1920.

Miles, Rufus E., Jr. *Awakening from the American Dream: The Social and Political Limits to Growth*. New York: Universe Books, 1977.

Milliband, Ralph. *The State in Capitalist Society*. New York: Basic, 1978.

Mill, John Stuart. *Considerations on Representative Government*. New York: Harper, 1862.

Miller, A.R. *Democratic Dictatorship*. Greenwood Press, 1980.

Momen, Moojan. *An Introduciton to Shii Islam*. New Haven: Yale University Press, 1985.

Niblock, Tim. *Iraq: The Contemporary State*. New York: St. Martin's Press, 1982.

Nonneman, Gerd. *Iraq, the Gulf States, and the War: A Changing Relationship, 1980-1986 and Beyond*. London: Ithaca Press, 1986.

Nordliner, E.H. *On the Autonomy of the Democratic State*. Cambridge, Massachusetts: Harvard University Press, 1981.

Nozick, Robert. *Anarchy, State and Utopia*. New York: Basic Books, Inc., 1974.

Odum, Howard D. *Environment, Power and Society*. New York: Wiley, 1971.

Olsen, William J. "Iraqi Policy and the Impact of the Iran-Iraq War." Pages 165-202 in Robert O. Freedman (ed.), *The Middle East After the Israeli Invasion of Lebanon*. Syracuse: Syracuse University Press, 1986.

Parenti, Michael. *Democracy for the Few*. 4th ed. New York: St. Martin's Press, 1983.

Partington, David H., ed. *The Middle East Annual: Issues and Events*. Vol. 5, 1985. Boston, Massachusetts: G.K. Hall & Co., 1985.

Pelletiere, Stephen C. *The Kurds: An Unstable Element in the Gulf*. Boulder, Colorado: Westview Press, 1984.

Penrose, Edith and E.F. Penrose. *Iraq: International Relations and National Development*. Boulder, Colorado: Westview Press, 1978.

Peretz, Don. *The Middle East Today*, 3rd ed. New York: Holt, Rinehart and Winston, 1978.

Phillips, Derek K. *Equality, Justice and Rectification: An Exploration in Normative Sociology*. London: Academic Press, 1979.

Plamenatz, John. *Democracy and Illusion*. New York: Longman, 1977.

Pyke, Magnus. *Our Future*. New York: Hamlin/America, 1980.

Quarles, John. *Cleaning Up America*. Boston: Houghton-Mifflin,

202/ Iraq and Democracy

1976.

Rae, D.W. *Equalities*. Cambridge, Massachusetts: Harvard University Press, 1981.

Ramazani, R.K. *Revolutionary Iran: Cahllenge and Response in the Middle East*. Baltimore: Johns Hopkins Univeristy Press, 1986.

Rand, Ayn. *The New Left: The Anti-Industrial Revolution*. New York: New American Library, 1971.

Reich, Bernard. *The Powers in the Middle East: The Ultimate Strategic Arena*. New York: Praeger, 1987.

Rezazadeh, Reza. *Technological Democracy: A Humanistic Philosophy of the Future Society*. New York: Vantage Press, 1990.

_____. *Technodemocratic Economic Theory: From Capitalism and Socialism to Democracy*. Platteville, Wisconsin: Eternalist Foundation, 1991.

Roux, George. *Ancient Iraq*. Cleveland: World Publishing, 1965.

Ryan, W. *Equality*. New York: Random House, 1982.

Sanford, Chalres L. *The Quest for Paradise: Europe and the American Moral Imagination*. Urbana: University of Illinois Press, 1961.

Schumacher, E.F. *Small is Beautiful*. New York: Harper and Row, 1973.

Schumpeter, Jospeh A. *Capitalism, Socialism, and Democracy*. New York: Harper and Row, 1950.

Schuster, Edward, *Human Rights Today: Evolution and Revolution*. New York: Philosophical Library, 1980.

Shwadran, Benjamin. *The Power Struggle in Iraq*. New York: Council for Middle Eastern Affairs Press, 1960.

Silver, Harold. *Equal Opportunity in Education*. New York: Methuen, Inc., 1979.

Simon, Reeva. *Iraq Between the Two World Wars*. New York: Columbia University Press, 1986.

Sinai, I. Robert. *The Decadence of the Modern World*. Cambridge, Massachusetts: Schenkman, 1977.

Stafford, Beer. *Designing Freedom*. New York: John Wiley and Sons, 1974.

Stafford, R.S. *The Tragedy of the Assyrians*. London: Allen and

Unwin, 1935.

Tahir-Kheli, Shirin, and Shaheen Ayubl (eds.) *The Iran-Iraq War: New Weapons, Old Conflicts*. New York: Praeger, 1983.

Thomas, Norman. *Democratic Socialism: A New Appraisal*. New York: League for Industrial Democracy, 1953.

Toynbee, Arnold. *Mankind and Mother Earth*. New York: Oxford University Press, 1976.

United States, Department of Commerce. International Trade Administration. *Foreign Economic Trends and Their Implications for the United States: Iraq* Washington: June 1986.

Usher, D. *The Economic Prerequisite to Democracy*. Boston: Columbia University Press, 1981.

Van Den Berghne, Peirre L. *Human Family Systems: An Evolutionary View*. Westport, Connecticut: Greenwood, n.d.

Wakim, Salim. *Iran, The Arabs, and the West*. New York: Vantage Press, 1987.

Weale, Albert. *Equality and Social Policy*. Boston: Rougledge and Kegan, 1978.

Welholt, F.M. *The Quest for Equality in Freedom*. New Brunswick, New Jersey: Transaction Books, 1979.

Westley, William A. *The Emerging Worker: Equality and Confilict in a Mass Consumption Society*. Downsview, Ontario: McGill-Queens Univeristy Press, 1971.

Weston, A.F. *Privacy and Freedom*. Bodley Head, 1967.

Wilensky, Harold I. *The Welfare State and Equality: Structural and Ideological Roots of Public Expenditures*. Berlkey: University of California Press, 1975.

Wilson, H.B. *Democracy and the Workplace*. Montreal: Black Rose Books, 1974.

Witte, J.F. *Democracy, Authority and Alienaiton in Work*. Chicago: University of Chicago Press, 1980.

Wolf, Alan. *The Limits of Legitimacy*. New York: Free Pres, 1977.

Wolgast, E.H. *Equality and the Rights of Women*. Ithaca: Cornell Univerisyt Press, 1980.

Articles and Documents

Abbas, A. "The Iraqi Armed Forces, Past and PResent." Pages 203 -226 in Committee Against Repressions and for Democratic Rights in Iraq (CARDI), (ed.), *Sadam's Iraq: Revolution or Reaction?* London: Zed Books, 1986.

Archibald, W.P. "Face to Face: The Alienating Effects of Class, Status and Power Divisions," *American Sociological Review 41.* (October 1976).

Baram, Amitzia. "The June 1980 Election to the National Assembly in Iraq," *Orient.* Vol. 27, No. 3, 1981.

Barry, B. "Political Accommodation and Consociational Democracy: Review Article," *British Journal of Political Science 5.* (October 1975).

Batatu, Hanna. "Iraq's Underground Shia Movement: Characteristics, Causes, and Prospects," *Middle East Journal.* Vol. 35, No. 4, Autumn 1981, 578-594.

_____. "Shi'i Organizations in Iraq: Al-Da'wah al-Islamiyah and Al-Mujahidin." Pages 179-200 in Juan R.I. Cole and Nikki R. Keddie (eds), *Shi'ism and Social Protest.* New Haven: Yale University Press, 1986.

Benn, A.W. "Democracy in the Age of Science," *Political Quarterly 50.* (January 1979), 7-23.

Bigler, C.S. "Tensions Between International Law and Strategic Security-Implications of Israel's Preemtive Raid on Iraq's Nuclear Reactor," *Virginia Journal of International Law.* Vol. 24, No. 2, 1984, 459-511.

Bill, James A. "Islam, Politics and Shi'ism in the Gulf, *Middle East Insight.* Vol 3, No. 3, January-February 1984, 3-12.

Birch, A.H. "Some Reflections on American Democratic Theory," *Political Studies 23.* (June/September 1975), 225-231.

Boulding, Kenneth E. "The Stability of Inequality," *Review of Social Economy 33.* No. 1 (April 1975), 1-14.

Bowles, Samuel, and Herbert Gintis. "The Crisis of Liberal Democratic Capitalism: The Case of the United States," *Politics and Society 1.* (1982), 51-93.

Brosnan, Peter. "Who Owns the Networks?" *Nation.* (November 25, 1978), 561, 577-579.

Brown, Michael E. "The Nationalizaiton of the Iraqi Petroleum Company," *International Journal of Middle East Studies*. Vol. 10, No. 1, Bebruary 1979, 107-124.

Cordesman, Anthony H. "The Attack on the USS Stark: The Tragic Cost of Human Error," *Armed Forces*. (London), Vol. 6, No. 10, October 1987, 447-450.

Coulson, Noel, and Doreen Hinchcliffe. "Women and Law Reform in Contemporary Islam." Pages 37-51 in Lois Beck and Nikki Keddie (eds.), *Women in the Muslim World*. Cambridge: Harvard University Press, 1978.

Dawisha, Adeed. "Iraq and the Arab World--The Gulf War and After," *World Today*, (London), Vol. 37, No. 5, May 1981, 188-194.

El-Azhary, M.S. "The Attitudes of the Superpowers Towards the Gulf War," *International Affairs*, (London), Vol. 59, No. 4, 1983, 609-620.

Entessar, Nader. "The Kurds in Post-Revolutionary Iran and Iraq," *World Quarterly*, (London), Vol. 6, No. 4, October 1984, 911-933.

Evans, David and Richard Campany. "Iran-Iraq: Bloody Tomarrows," *United States Naval Institute Proceedings*, Vol. 111, No. 1, January 1985, 33-43.

Fave Della, L.R. "In the Structure of Egalitarianism," *Social Problems 22*. (December 1974), 199-213.

Gabbay, Rony. "Iraq: The Search for Stability," *Conflict Studies*. (London), Vol. 59, July 1975, 1-22.

Ghareeb, Edmund. "Iraq and Gulf Security." Pages 39-64 in Z. Michael Szaz (ed.), *The Impact of the Iranian Events Upon Persian Gulf and United States Securiity*. Washington: American Foriegn Policy Institute, 1979.

_____. "Iraq: Emergent Gulf Power." Pages 197-230 in Hossein Amirsadeghi (ed.), *The Security of the Persian Gulf*. New York: St. Martin's Press, 1981.

Gotlieb, Yosef. "Sectarianism and the Iraqi State." Pages 153-161 in Michael Curtis (ed.), *Religion and Politics in the Middle East*. Boulder, Colorado: Westview Press, 1981.

Green, Philip, and Robert A. Dahl. "What is Political Equality?" *Dissent 26*. (Summer 1979), 352-368.

Grove, D.J. "Ethnic Socio-Economic Redistribution: A Cross-Cultural
    Study," *Comparative Politics 12*. (October 1979), 87-98.
Gruemm, H. "Safeguards and Tamuz: Setting the Record Straight,"
    International Atomic Energy Agency Bulletin. (VIenna), Vol.
    23, No. 4, December 1981, 10-14.
"Gulf War Moves Towards the Final Showdown," *Middle East
    Economic Digest*. (London), Vol. 31, No. 51, December 19,
    1987, 32-33.
Halliday, Fred. "The USSR and the Gulf War: Moscow's Growing
    Concern." Pages 10-11 in MERIP, *Middle East Report*. No.
    148, September-October 1987. Washington: Middle East
    Research Information Project.
Hanes, D. "Democracy in the Service of Peace and Man," *World
    Marx Review 19*. (April 1976), 56-66.
Heilbroner, Robert. "The Human Prospect: Second Thoughts,"
    Futures 7. (1975), 31-40.
Heller, Agnes. "Past, Present, and Future of Democracy," *Social
    Research 45*. (Winter 1978), 866-886.
Helms, "The Iraqi Dilemma: Political Objectives Versus Military
    Strategy," *American-Arab Affairs*. No. 5, September 1983,
    76-85.
Hewitt, C. "Effect of Political Democracy on Equality in Industrial
    Societies: A Cross-National Comparison," *American Social
    Review 42*. (June 1977), 450-464. "Discussion," 44, 168-
    172; 45, 344-349 (February 1979, April 1980).
Hodgson, Marshall G.S. "How Did the Early Shia Become
    Sectarian?"*Journal of the American Oriental Society*, Vol. 75,
    No. 1, January-March 1955, 1-13.
Hoivik, Tord. "Social Inequality--the Main Issues," *Journal of Peace
    Research 7*. No. 2, (1971), 119-141.
Howe, I. "Seasons for Democracy," *Dissent 21*. (Fall 1974), 460
    -470.
Hutchins, R.M. "Is Democracy Possible?" *Center Magazine 9*.
    (January 1976), 2-6.
Hyneman, Charles S. "Equality: Elusive Ideal or Beguiling
    Delusion?" *Modern Age 24*. No. 3, (Summer 1980), 226-
    237.

"Iraq." Pages 465-477 in *The Middle East and North Africa, 1989*. London: Europa Publications, 1988.

Iueller, D.C. "Constitutional Democracy and Social Welfare," *Quarterly Journal of Economics 87*. (February 1973), 60-80.

Jackman, R.W. "Political Democracy and Social Equality: A Comparative Analysis," *American Sociological Review 39*. (February 1974), 29-45.

Kedourie, Elie. "Continuity and Change in Modern Iraqi History," *Asian Affairs*. (London), June 1975, 140-146.

Kelidar, Abbas. "Iraq: The Search for Stability," *Conflict Studies*. (London), Vol. 59, July 1975, 1-22.

Kellner, M.M. "Democracy and Civil Disobedience," *Journal of Politics 37*. (November 1975), 899-916.

Kelly, J., and H.S. Klein. "Revolution and the Rebirth of Inequality: A Theory of Stratification in Post-Revolutionary Scoiety," *American Journal of Sociology 83*. (July 1977), 78-98.

Kempe, Frederick. "Badhdad's Goal: Iraq's Aim in Gulf War is No Longer to Win But to Avoid Losing," *Wall Street Journal*. August 28, 1987, 1, 14.

Al-Khafaji, Isam. "State Incubation of Iraqi Capitalism." Pages 4-12 in *MERIP Middle East Report*, No. 142, September-October 1986, Washington: Middle East Research and Information Project.

Kishida, Junnosuke. "Civilized Society: In Search of New Forms." *Impact of Science on Society 30*. No. 2, (1980), 101-109.

Laird, R. "Post-Industrial Scoeity: East and West," *Survey 21*. (Autumn 1975), 1-17.

Lemos, R.M. "Moral Argument for Democracy," *Social Theory and Practice 4*. (Fall 1976), 57-74.

Levin, M.F. "Equality of Opportunity," *Philosophical Quarterly 31*. (April 1981), 110-125, 25-26.

Livingston, David, and Richard Masson. "Ecological Crisis and the Autonomy of Science in Capitalist Society: The Canadian Case Study," *Alternatives 8*. (1977), 3-19.

Lowenthal, R. "Social Transformation and Democratic Legitimacy," *Social Research 43*. (Summer 1976), 241-275.

Lukes, S. "Socialism and Equality," *Dissent 22*. (Spring 1975), 154 -168.

Lustick, I. "Stability in Deeply Divided Societies: Consociationism Versus Control," *World Politics 31* (April 1979), 325-344.

Marr, Phebe. "The Political Elite in Iraq." Pages 109-149 in George Lenczowski (ed.), *Political Elites in the Middle East.* Washington: American Enterprose Institute, 1975.

McBride, W.L. "Concept of Justic in Marx, Engels, and Others,: *Ethics 85.* (April 1975), 204-218.

McDermott, John. "Technology: The Opiate of the Intellecturals." In Albert H. Teich (ed.), *Technology and Man's Future*, 4th ed., New York: St. Martin's Press, 1981, 95-121.

Mankoff, Milton. "Toward Socialism: Reassessing Inequality," *Social Policy 4.* (March 1974), 20-31.

Margolis, J. "Political Equality and Political Justice," *Social Research.* (Summer 1977), 308-329.

Miller, D. "Democracy and Social Justice," *British Journal of Sociology 8.* (January 1978), 1-19.

Neubauer, Deane E. "Some Condisitons of Democracy," *American Political Science Review 61*, (December 1967), 1007-1009.

Nielson, K. "Impediments to Radical Egalitarianism," *American Philisophical Quarterly 18.* (April 1980), 121-129.

Nixon, C.R. "Equity, Identity, and Social Cleavage: Cross-Cultural Perspectives," *American Behavioral Scientists 18.* (Summer 1984), 4-14.

North, J. "Landscape of Equality," *Times Literary Supplement 4088.* (August 7, 1981), 903-904.

Olson, William J. "iraqi Policy and the Impact of the Iran-Iraq War." Pages 165-202 in Robert O. Freedman (ed.), *The Middle East After the Israeli Invasion of Lebanon.* Syracuse: Syracuse University Press, 1986.

Owen, D. "Communism, Socialism and Democracy," *Atlantic Community Quarterly 16.* (Summer 1978), 154-166.

Piskinov, A.I. "The Soviet School and Soviet Pedagogy in the Period of the Competition of Socitalist Construction and Gradual Transition to Communism," *Soviet Education.* (February 1977), 71-75.

Pyatt, G. "On International Comparisons of Inequality," *American Economic Review: Papers and Proceedings 67.* (February 1977), 71-75.

Renfrew, Nita M. "Who Started the War?" *Foreign Policy*. No. 66, Spring 1987, 98-108.

Robinson, R.V., and W. Bell. "Equality, Success, and Social Justice in England and the United States," *American Sociological Review 43*. (April 1978), 328-329.
A.C. Kerckhoff and R.N. Parker, "Reply with Rejoinder." 44 (April 1979), 328-339.

Rubinson, R., and D. Quinlan. "Democracy and Social Inequality: A Reanalysis," *American Sociological Review 42*, (August 1977), 611-623.

Rodman, John. "The Liberation of Nature?" *Inquiry 20*. (1977), 83 -131.

Schonfield, W.R. "Meaning of Democratic Participation," *World Politics 28*. (October 1978), 134-158.

Sciolino, Elaine. "The Big Brother: Iraq Under Saddam Hussein," *New York Times Magazine*. February 3, 1985, 16.

Simpson, E. "Socialist Justice," *Ethics 87*, (October 1976), 1-17.

Sinal, I.R. "What Ails Us and Why?" *Encounter 52*. (April 1979), 8-17. "Discussion," Vol. 54, (February 1980), 87-93.

Sluglett, Peter. "The Kurds." Pages 177-202 in Committee Against Repression and for Democratic Rights in Iraq (CARDRI), (ed.), *Saddam's Iraq: Revolution or Reaction?* London: Zed Books, 1986.

Stack, S. "Political Economy of Income Inequallity: A Comparative Analysis," *Canadian Journal of Political Science 13*. (June 1980), 273-286.

"Syrians, Iraqis Bury Hatchet, but Not in Iran," *Iran Times*. Vol. 17, No. 35, November 13, 1984, 15-16.

Thompson, K.W. "American Democracy and the Third World: Convergence and Contradictions," *Review of Politics*. Vol. 41, (April 1979), 256-272.

Thurow, L. "Pursuit of Equity," *Dissent 23*. (Summer 1976), 253 -259.

Tonsor, S.J. "Liberty and Equality as Absolutes," *Modern Age 23*. (Winter 1979), 2-9.
_____. "New Natural Law and the Problem of Equality," *Modern Age 24*. (Summer 1980), 238-247.

Tyree, A. "Gapo and Glissandos: Inequality, Economic Development, and Social Mobility in 24 Countries," *American Sociological Review 44.* (June 1979), 410-424.

Vanly, I.C. "Kurdistan in Iraq." Pages 192-203 in Gerard Chaliand (ed.), *People Without a Country: The Kurds and Kurdistan.* London: Zed Books, 1980.

Viorst, Milton. "Iraq at War," *Foreign Affairs 65.* No. 2, Winter 1986-1987, 349-365.

Zaher, U. "Political Developments in Iran, 1963-1980." Pages 30-53 in Committee Against Repression and for Democratic Rights in Iraq (CARDRI), (ed.), *Saddam's Iraq: Revolution or Reaction?* London: Zed Books, 1986.

Zetterbaum, M. "Equality and Human Need," *American Political Science Review 71.* (September 1977), 983-998.

Index

108, 109-114, 122, 129,
131, 181-183
Procedural democracy 5, 140, 141,
143, 145
Profit 131, 135, 136
Progressive National Front 41
Provisional Constitution 30, 37,
38, 42, 44, 46, 47
Public Service Council 48
Quraysh 11-13
Regional Command 39, 41, 44, 46,
48, 68
Republicanism 3, 28
Revolutionary Command Council
3, 4, 30, 41, 44, 46, 48, 90,
91-95, 177
Revolutionary Court 50
Revolutionary Guard 33
Revolutionary socialism 42
Saddam Hussein 29-35, 38, 39, 41,
47, 48, 51, 68, 69, 176, 177,
178, 209
Salary range 168
Saudi Arabia 3, 6, 7, 32, 35, 68,
72, 85, 171-175, 184
Secret police 41, 51, 69
Semetic 6, 7, 20, 21
Senate 4, vii, 96, 101, 102, 104,
108, 111, 112, 114
Shah of Iran 29, 31
Shared opportunity 5, 145, 157,
158, 159
Shatt al Arab 33
Shias 3, 22-24, 26-28, 32, 33, 69,
74, 76, 78, 79, 86, 173, 174,
176, 179
Singapore viii, 62-64
Social justice vii, viii, 199, 208,
209
Socialistic 4, 32, 96, 132, 151, 175
Socialization 39, 140
Socioeconomic development 4, 56,
57, 62, 65, 66, 70, 71, 130
South Korea viii, 54, 56, 57
Suharto 64
Sumarians 20

Sumer 19, 20
Sunnis 3, 22, 24, 27, 28
Supreme Court vi, 49, 103, 108,
112, 113, 114, 118, 123, 130
Syria 3, 5, 6, 8, 9, 11, 26, 32, 38,
39, 54, 88, 173, 174, 176,
184
Taiwan viii, 63, 64
The Arab Nation 37
Tikrit 30, 41
Trade unions 29, 59
Tribunal of Administrative Justice
114
Turkey vi, 3, 5, 7, 9, 26, 54, 56,
57, 58, 88, 171, 173, 190
Turkish language 7
U.S. Constitution vi, 118
U.S. Supreme Court vi, 49, 118
UN Security Council 178, 179
Unfair accumulation 151
United National Front 38
United Republics of Iraq 4, 70, 96,
99, 102-104, 107, 108, 115,
116, 127, 179, 182, 183, 184
Unjust enrichment 5, 145, 147,
150
Vice president 90, 92, 101, 107,
108
Vote of confidence 100, 101, 110
Voting Rights Act v
Western power 65
Western values v, viii
Work system 159, 166
Writ of Habeas Corpus 106
Young Turks 25
Zakah 17
Ziggurat 20
Zoroastrians vi, 99